WOW!
This is Low Cholesterol
and Sugarfree

Artwork by Mary Yoder

ISBN 0-9711105-2-2

For more copies contact:
Apple View Publications
4495 Cutter Road
Apple Creek, OH 44606-9641

2673 TR 421
Sugarcreek, OH 44681

Carlisle Printing
WALNUT CREEK

~Acknowledgments~

Our sincere thanks to all of the special people who contributed of their time and talent in making this book a reality.

To Diane for doing the typesetting and graphics for this manuscript.

To Darla, Dorisa, and Danae for trying and retrying recipes until they were just right.

To Brian Yoder for the many hours of time spent in proofreading the manuscript.

To our husbands for their patience and encouragement when the task seemed impossible. Also for tasting our many creations and giving their honest and occasionally painful opinions.

And finally, to all of you who have enjoyed our cookbooks and have been so gracious as to write or call to let us know you have appreciated our efforts. You have given us the encouragement we needed to delve into the task of producing our latest cookbook.

We trust this book will be helpful to all who are searching for a genuinely healthy way of eating.

Thank you all!
Deborah Steiner and Mary Yoder

~ Introduction ~

Are you concerned about the future of your family's health?

The typical American diet consists mainly of red meat, rich desserts, and convenience foods high in fat, sugar, and salt.

There are many today who have not learned to cook because it is so complicated and time consuming. But as we study nutrition and the effect refined foods have on our bodies, cooking can become enjoyable and purposeful. You have probably heard the statement, "you are what you eat". That is very true. Food affects who we are, how we feel, and how we respond to various situations. It affects our energy level and our overall health.

Are you tired of restrictive diets that you can't stick to? The problem with many such diets is that people become weary of them and give up. Our aim is to provide you with a wide variety of delicious, nutritious foods.

Because of my concern for my husband's health, I have been following a low-cholesterol and sugar free way of cooking for many years. With a family history of diabetes and heart problems, and his mother having open-heart surgery, I felt we needed a healthier diet to avoid future problems.

If you, like me are concerned about your family's health, but hate to hear comments like: "What's this stuff?". "If this is what we're having, I'm going out to eat". "Why can't we have good food anymore?" or "What happened to normal food?", take courage. Your family will thank you eventually. They will in time realize that they feel better and are sick less frequently.

Taste buds vary and many people need to acquire a taste for healthy, unrefined foods. Give your family and yourself time. If they are hesitant to try these new foods, start by using part white and part whole grain flours, using less white and more whole grain, until you are using all whole grain flour.

One half the amount of sugar can be used and half stevia, gradually decreasing to one fourth sugar and three fourths stevia, until you are using all stevia. Only make one new food per meal.

We wish you success on your journey in healthy cooking.

Deborah Steiner

~Before You Begin~

Some of our recipes ask for "malt sweetened carob chips". The reason for that is because unsweetened carob chips don't melt. Malt sweetened carob chips sweetened with barley malt are delicious and can be used for all the recipes calling for carob chips. However if you are unable to use barley malt, unsweetened carob chips are ideal for cookies and bars.

We use whole grains and whole grain products because they are more nutritious. Refined products have the bran and germ removed to give them a longer shelf life. Most of the nutrients are in the bran and germ. Since whole grain products are more perishable, be sure to keep them refrigerated or frozen unless instructed otherwise in the recipes.

Choose a salt that is unrefined. See page VII for more salt information.

We prefer Stevia herb which is green, for a sweetener, rather than the more refined Stevia extract. See page 196 for more information on stevia.

Do you have food in your refrigerator that gets a fuzzy mold because you didn't get it used? See page 204 for recipes in which to use leftovers.

When we have two ingredients listed such as "juice" or "water", the first one listed is preferable. If you don't have the first ingredient or need to avoid it, use the second option.

Many of our recipes ask you to "saute". To saute, heat the skillet over medium-high heat. Add olive oil to skillet spreading over entire bottom of skillet. Add ingredients called for, stirring for 2 - 3 minutes or as directed.

~Before You Begin *(Continued)* ~

Always read over the recipe before beginning, to be sure you have all the ingredients and avoid surprises.

When baking, always preheat the oven and grease the pan before combining ingredients.

Be sure to level your ingredients in measuring cups, Tbsp., and tsp.

There are "good" cholesterols called HDLs and there are "bad" cholesterols called LDLs. **The best oil to use is olive oil** and should be used as your main oil. It is high in heart-healthy monounsaturated fats that can help to lower the LDLs and raise the HDLs.

Refined sugars in your diet cause the saturated fats and cholesterol you eat to raise the serum cholesterol and triglycerides.

High fat diets contribute to colon, prostate and breast cancer, obesity, arteriosclerosis, strokes, and heart attacks.

Canola oil has had some bad publicity on the Internet on the dangers of using it as a food. We suggest you re-search the subject and make your decisions based on what you find. To be safe, we have decided to no longer use it, although we had used it in "WOW! This Is Sugar Free" and "WOW! This Is Allergy Free". Olive oil can be used instead of canola oil and is good for you.

Eat lots of raw foods. A good rule is to eat at least one raw food per meal. The closer we eat our foods to the way God made them, the more nourishing they are.

~Stocking The Pantry~

 Most of these items can be found at food co-ops, health food stores, bulk food stores, or check in the "Resources" section for suppliers.

Carob Chips: Carob Chips are either unsweetened or malt sweetened. Unsweetened Carob Chip ingredients are: carob, partially hydrogenated vegetable oil, and soy lecithin (an emulsifier). Malt Sweetened Carob Chip ingredients are: barley malt (malt, corn), partially hydrogenated palm kernel oil, carob, and soy lecithin. For melting, use malt sweetened carob chips.

Carob Powder: Carob is a healthy substitute for chocolate. Chocolate can deplete our organs and cells of minerals causing cravings and overeating. Carob is high in calcium and trace minerals.

Fruit Juice Sweetened Corn Flakes: Very low in salt.

Gelatin: Plain or unflavored gelatin can be used in place of Jello. Use 1 Tbsp. in place of one small box of Jello and use fruit juice in place of water.

Grains: The various grains are available from food co-ops, health food stores, or you may be able to obtain them from a local farmer at a considerable savings and grind your own flour.

~*Stocking The Pantry* (Continued)~

Olive Oil: As a rule we use olive oil. If you don't like olive oil, gradually add and increase the amount of olive oil as you learn to appreciate the taste. Olive oil contains oleic acid, which is a mono unsaturated fat. Oleic acid is an antioxidant, and also tends to lower blood pressure, and help regulate blood sugar levels. Some people need to rotate brands occasionally to avoid intolerance.

Buy "Extra Virgin, Cold Pressed" olive oil. It is pressed from the olive fruit. Olive oil labeled "pomace" or "contains pomace" is made by extracting oil (usually chemically) from the pits and leftover pulp after the first two pressings. It may be inexpensive, but it is not worth buying, as the flavor is not as good, and the health benefits have been mostly removed.

Some brands we use are: **Bertolli, Golden Barrel, Marconi, Omaggio, and Spectrum.**
(See page 187-190 for "Bad Fats" and "Good Fats")

Peanut Butter: We use pure peanut butter containing only peanuts. Commercially prepared peanut butter contains dextrose, corn syrup, and hydrogenated oils. Keep refrigerated.

Rice Milk: Milk substitute for those allergic to milk or avoiding milk due to cholesterol problems.

Rice Dream Nondairy Dessert: Substitute for ice cream with no sugar or artificial sweeteners, and can be found in health food stores and food co-ops.

~Stocking The Pantry (Continued)~

Orange and Lemon Peel: Grate your own, or to avoid spray and dyes, purchase it in your local health food store or co-op.

Salt: <u>Celtic Sea Salt</u> is a naturally moist salt containing a balanced mixture of essential minerals. Because of the moisture, it works best added to liquid and stirred to dissolve. (We like it for everything except baking.) Some people required to be on a salt free diet find they are able to use Celtic salt in moderation. For more information, or to order, call 1-800-867-7258 or www.celtic-seasalt.com.

<u>Real Salt:</u> a natural mineral sea salt with no chemicals added. It has not been heated or cooked in processing. (We use this salt for baking.) Can be found in bulk food, food co-op, or health food stores or www.realsalt.com

<u>Bio Salt:</u> a fine textured salt found in health food stores. Some persons required to be on a salt free diet also find that they can use small amounts of this salt.
See page 192-194 for <u>Adjusting to Less or No Salt</u>.

Stevia: (Stevia Rebaudiana). Stevia is a plant in the daisy family, grows naturally in South America, and can be used as an herbal sweetener. Stevia can be found in your food co-op or health food store, or about anywhere that herbs are sold.
See page 196 for more information on stevia.
For <u>Stevia Conversion Chart</u> see page VIII.

~ Charts ~

WEIGHTS AND MEASURES

3 teaspoons = 1 tablespoon
12 teaspoons = ¼ cup
4 tablespoons = ¼ cup
5⅓ tablespoons = ⅓ cup
8 tablespoons = ½ cup
10⅔ tablespoons = ⅔ cup
12 tablespoons = ¾ cup
14 tablespoons = ⅞ cup
16 tablespoons = 1 cup
2 tablespoons = 1 liquid ounce
1 cup = ½ pint
2 cups = 1 pint
4 cups = 1 quart
4 quarts = 1 gallon
8 quarts = 1 peck
4 pecks = 1 bushel
16 ounces = 1 pound

ABBREVIATIONS

Tbsp. = tablespoon
tsp. = teaspoon
oz. = ounce
lb. = pound
qt. = quart
w/ = with

SUBSTITUTIONS

1 Tbsp. cornstarch = 2 Tbsp. flour or
1½ Tbsp. quick cooking tapioca

1 tsp. baking powder = ¼ tsp. baking soda +
½ tsp. cream of tartar

1 oz. unsweetened baking chocolate =
3 Tbsp. carob powder + 2 Tbsp. olive oil or
fruit juice concentrate

COOKED FOOD MEASUREMENTS

1 cup uncooked rice = 3 cups cooked
⅓ cup uncooked lentils = 1 cup cooked

STEVIA CONVERSION CHART

Sugar	Stevia Herb (green)	Liquid Stevia
1 cup	1 tsp.	1 tsp.
1 Tbsp.	⅛ tsp.	6 drops
1 tsp.	pinch	2 drops

Fruit Source & Barley Malt	Stevia Herb (green)	Liquid Stevia
¼ cup	1 tsp.	1 tsp.

Note: Stevia Extract (white) varies in sweetness.
Try one-half or less of the amount you would use of the Stevia Herb (green).

~Table of Contents~

~Table of Contents *(Continued)*~

Breakfasts
and
Beverages

APPLE STREUSEL

STREUSEL

In small bowl, combine:
1/2 cup rolled oats
1/4 cup whole grain flour
1/2 tsp. stevia
3 Tbsp. olive oil

Set aside.

In mixer bowl, lightly beat:
1 egg

Add:
1 cup whole grain flour
1/2 cup rolled oats
1 tsp. baking powder
1/4 tsp. salt
1 cup milk or water

Mix until just combined.
Set batter aside.

Combine in small bowl:
3 medium apples, peeled and cut in thin wedges
1 tsp. cinnamon
1/4 tsp. nutmeg

Place apples in bottom of greased 8 x 8" baking pan.
Spoon batter over apples.
Sprinkle streusel over top.
Bake 350° F. for 40 minutes.
Serve warm or cold.

COCONUT FRENCH TOAST

8 slices whole grain bread

In mixing bowl, beat:
8 eggs
1/2 cup milk or rice milk
1/4 tsp. stevia
3/4 tsp. cinnamon
pinch salt

Soak each slice of bread, one at a time, for 1 minute.
Coat both sides with unsweetened, shredded coconut.
Place on greased baking sheet.
Bake 475° F. for 5 minutes on each side.　　　　　Serves 4

Variation:
Sprinkle slivered almonds over bread before turning to second side.

GRANOLA

Combine in large bowl:
6 cups rolled oats
1 cup oat bran
1/2 cup almonds, sliced or slivered
1/2 cup finely chopped walnuts
1/2 cup flaked, unsweetened coconut
1/2 tsp. stevia

Mix together and add:
1/4 cup olive oil
1/3 cup white grape juice concentrate or apple juice concentrate
1 1/2 tsp. vanilla

Bake 325° F. for 30 minutes or until lightly toasted,
stirring every 10 - 15 minutes.

Add:
1 1/2 cups raisins

Tip:
Try granola sprinkled over ice cream.

Tip:
Add a little olive oil to granola and use for pie crumb topping. Bake as usual.

OMELET

Frying eggs increases the harmful effects of eggs on the body.
Try this delicious baked omelet.

FILLING

In a large skillet, saute in 1 Tbsp. olive oil until tender:
1 onion, chopped
1 bell pepper, chopped
3 mushrooms, chopped

Add:
3 small zucchini, chopped
1 tomato, chopped
$1/4$ tsp. oregano
$1/4$ tsp. salt
$1/8$ tsp. pepper

Note: Browned sausage and hash browns can be added
or substituted for zucchini.

Saute 4 minutes longer.
Set aside and keep warm.

OMELETS

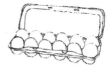

Beat until peaks form:
8 egg whites (place yolks in blender)
$1/2$ cup water
$1/2$ tsp. cream of tartar

Process yolks in blender and fold yolks into egg whites.
Divide into 4 - 9" greased pie pans or baking dishes.
Bake 350° F. for 12 - 15 minutes or until knife inserted in center
comes out clean.
Divide filling onto omelets, covering half of it.
Sprinkle cheese over top.
Cut partway through middle and fold over.

Yields 4 omelets, or cut in half for 8 omelets

BREAKFAST PIZZA
(Delicious for any meal)

Prepare pizza crust and prebake. (page 49)

HASH BROWNS

In skillet, brown in 2 Tbsp. olive oil:
4 cups cooked, shredded potatoes

Add:
1/2 tsp. chili powder
1/4 tsp. salt

Remove from pan and set aside.

Beat:
7 large eggs
1/2 cup water
1/2 tsp salt

Set aside.

In the same skillet, saute in 1 Tbsp. olive oil:
1 small onion, chopped
1 Tbsp. chopped pepper
1 garlic clove, minced

Add eggs, cook, and stir until almost set.
Remove from heat.

Spread over crust:
1 cup salsa

Spread eggs over salsa.
Sprinkle with hash browns.
Top with cheese, if desired.
Bake 375° F. for 10 minutes.

**Eat lots
of fruits and
vegetables.**
They are a great
source of fiber, have
little fat, and no
cholesterol!

PIZZA EGGS

Beat:

5 eggs   ⅛ cup milk or rice milk

Pour into greased 9" pie pan.
Bake 325° F. for 25 minutes or until set.

Hint:
Ask your butcher to process bologna, sausage, and wieners, without sugar or MSG. Ask him to just add the spices such as salt, pepper, mustard, and garlic.

Spread over top:
¾ cup pizza sauce

Top with toppings of your choice:

browned ground beef   onions
sausage   mushrooms
grated bologna or wieners   olives
peppers   cheese, etc.

Return to oven to bake until cheese is melted.   Serves 3

EGGS IN A NEST

(Children love this for a breakfast or lunch treat)

Lightly oil large heated skillet.
Cut a 2 inch circle in the middle of each slice of bread.
Place slices, single layer, in skillet over low heat.
Break one egg into each hole.
Season with salt and pepper.

When egg is almost set, carefully turn over for just a little bit.
Place right side up on serving plate.

HARD COOKED EGGS

Bring water to a boil.
With a large spoon, carefully drop eggs in water, one at a time.
Cover and cook for 10 - 15 minutes.
Cool under cold water.

OVERNIGHT BUCKWHEAT PANCAKES

Combine in mixer bowl:

1 cup warm water
2 Tbsp. white grape juice concentrate, warm
1 Tbsp. yeast

Allow to soak 5 minutes.

Meanwhile, process in blender:

$^1/_2$ cup water
$^1/_4$ cup dates

Pour into mixer bowl.

Add:

1$^1/_2$ cups whole grain flour
1$^1/_2$ cups buckwheat flour
1 tsp. salt

Cover and refrigerate.

Next morning, add:

$^1/_4$ cup olive oil
1 tsp. baking soda dissolved in:
$^1/_2$ cup very warm water

Allow to set at room temperature 30 minutes. (I don't always)
Pour onto hot, greased griddle or heavy skillet.
Turn pancakes once.   Serves 6

WHOLE GRAIN PANCAKES

Beat:

2 eggs   1 tsp. lemon juice
3 Tbsp. olive oil

Add:

1$^3/_4$ cups whole grain flour $^1/_2$ tsp. salt
1 tsp. stevia   1$^1/_2$ cups water
2 tsp. baking powder

Mix until just combined.
Pour batter onto hot, greased griddle or heavy skillet.
Turn pancakes once.   Serves 4

Pancake syrup is high in sugar and calories. Make your own fruit pancake topping, spread with unsweetened peanut butter, or eat plain, fresh off the griddle.

OATMEAL WAFFLES

In mixer bowl, beat:

3 Tbsp. olive oil

3 Tbsp. apple sauce

2 eggs

Add:

1 1/2 cups whole grain flour

1 Tbsp. baking powder

1/2 tsp. cinnamon

1 tsp. stevia

1/4 tsp. salt

1 1/2 cups apple juice or water

Mix until just combined.

Fold in:

1 cup rolled oats

Pour batter onto preheated, lightly greased waffle iron.　　Serves 4

Oat **bran** is a valuable tool for lowering your cholesterol. Sprinkle some over your hot or cold cereal.

PANCAKE TOPPING

Bring to a boil:

1/2 cup water

1 quart blueberries or raspberries

Stir together in measuring cup:

2 Tbsp. corn starch

1/2 cup white grape juice concentrate or 1/2 cup water and 1 tsp. stevia

1/4 tsp grated lemon peel

While stirring, pour juice into boiling berries.

Continue stirring and cooking for 2 minutes.

Serve over pancakes or waffles.　　Serves 8

SPICED APPLE CIDER

Welcome guests with the wonderful aroma of this delicious drink.

Place in crock pot:

4 cups apple cider

2 cups pineapple juice

1 - 3 inch cinnamon stick

1 tsp. whole cloves

1/4 tsp. allspice

Cover and cook on low for 2 1/2 hours or until desired temperature.

Discard cloves and cinnamon stick before serving.

HOT CAROB BEVERAGE

Add approximately 2 Tbsp. Carob Ice Cream Topping. (page 158)
to 1 cup hot milk or rice milk.
Stir and enjoy!

CITRUS REFRESHER

To sweeten tea:
Brew whole or crushed stevia leaves with the tea leaves.

In blender, process until smooth:
1 cup cold water
2 ripe bananas
1 cup whole strawberries
3/4 cup orange juice concentrate

Add:
3 cups pineapple juice

Stir and pour into glasses.

Serves 6 - 8

TANGY FRUIT DRINK

Your guests will enjoy this refreshing unsweetened drink.

Combine:
1 can frozen pineapple juice concentrate
1 can frozen orange juice concentrate
1/4 cup lemon juice
6 cups water

In blender, process until smooth:
2 cups whole, frozen strawberries, partially thawed
1 ripe banana
1 cup water

Stir into fruit juice. Chill.

Tip:
For guests and special occasions we add club soda, (which is carbonated water with no sweeteners added) to fruit juice.

Just before serving, add:
2 cups club soda, chilled

Serves 12

FLOATING ORANGE JUICE

Chill grape juice.
Freeze orange juice in ice cube trays.
To serve, put orange juice cubes into grape juice.
Looks pretty in clear glasses.

STRAWBERRY LEMONADE

(Pictured on front cover)

In blender, process until smooth:
3 cups cold water
1 quart whole strawberries
$^1/_2$ tsp. stevia
$^1/_2$ cup lemon juice
$^1/_4$ cup white grape juice concentrate

Just before serving, add 2 cups chilled club soda.
Garnish with thinly sliced lemon if desired.   Serves 6 - 8

FLU TEA

Many health food stores and food co-ops have herbs in bulk.

Combine in a tightly covered container or 2 gallon ziploc bag:
12 oz. peppermint
4 oz. red clover
4 oz. raspberry
2 oz. comfrey
2 oz. echinacea
1 oz. elder
$^1/_4$ oz. nettle
$^1/_4$ oz. yarrow
2 oz. stevia leaves

Try squeezing fresh lemon into your tea for a tangy refreshing treat.

Place $^3/_4$ - 1 cup in 12 cup coffee maker.
Stir each time before using as the stevia tends to settle to the bottom.

Note: To be sure tea is equally sweet each time, omit stevia from mixture. Add 1$^1/_2$ tsp. stevia per pot of tea.

Breads

BISCUITS

In a bowl, combine:

2 cups whole grain flour
2 tsp. baking powder
$^1/_2$ tsp. cream of tartar

$^1/_2$ tsp. baking soda
$^1/_2$ tsp. salt
$^1/_4$ cup olive oil

Add:

$^3/_4$ cup water

Mix until just combined.
Drop onto greased cookie sheet.
Bake 450° F. for 15 minutes.

Yields 10 biscuits

GARLIC BISCUITS

In mixer bowl, combine:

2 cups whole grain flour
4 tsp. baking powder
1 tsp. cream of tartar

$^1/_4$ tsp. garlic powder
$^1/_8$ tsp. salt
3 Tbsp. olive oil

Add:

$^7/_8$ cup water

Mix just until combined. Immediately drop biscuits on cookie sheet.
Bake 375° F. for 12 minutes.

Yields 12 biscuits

SWEET POTATO BISCUITS

Beat:

2 Tbsp. olive oil

1 cup cooked, mashed, sweet potatoes

Add:

2$^3/_4$ cups whole grain flour
4 tsp. baking powder

$^1/_2$ tsp. salt
$^1/_4$ tsp. stevia, opt.

Mix slightly, then quickly add:

$^3/_4$ cup water.

Mix just until combined.
Immediately drop by spoonfuls onto cookie sheet.
Bake 400° F. for 15 minutes.

Yields 15 biscuits

APPLE SAUCE MUFFINS

In mixer bowl beat:
1 egg
1 cup apple sauce

$^1/_4$ cup apple butter

Add:
2 cups whole grain flour
2 tsp. baking powder
$^3/_4$ tsp. baking soda

$^3/_4$ tsp. cinnamon
$^1/_4$ tsp. nutmeg
$^1/_2$ tsp. stevia

Mix until just combined.

Fold in:
$^3/_4$ cup raisins

Fill greased muffin tin.
Bake 375° F. for 25 minutes.

Yields 12 muffins

APPLE WALNUT MUFFINS

Beat:
2 eggs

Add:
2$^1/_4$ cups whole grain flour
3 Tbsp. oat bran
1 tsp. baking soda
$^1/_2$ tsp. cinnamon
$^1/_4$ tsp. ginger

$^1/_4$ tsp. nutmeg
$^1/_4$ tsp. allspice
$^1/_2$ tsp. salt
1$^2/_3$ cups apple juice

Mix until just combined.

Fold in:
3 medium, peeled Yellow Delicious apples, finely chopped
$^1/_2$ cup chopped walnuts

Use sweet apples rather than tart in recipes. We prefer Yellow or Golden Delicious.

Spoon batter into greased muffin tins, filling almost full.
Place an apple slice on top of each muffin.
Bake 375° F. for 25 minutes.

Yields about 15 muffins

BANANA NUT MUFFINS

In mixer bowl, beat:

2 eggs
2 large ripe bananas

$\frac{1}{2}$ cup olive oil
1 tsp. vanilla

Add:

2 cups whole grain flour
1 tsp. salt
1 tsp. baking powder

$\frac{1}{2}$ tsp. baking soda
$\frac{1}{2}$ tsp. stevia
1 cup apple juice or water

Mix until just combined.

Fold in:

$\frac{1}{2}$ cup chopped pecans

Spoon batter into greased muffin tins, filling almost full.
Bake 400° F. for 20 minutes.   Yields 18 muffins

Note:
If you don't have enough batter to fill each muffin cup, fill empty cups half full with water to prevent a warped pan.

BUCKWHEAT MUFFINS

In mixer bowl, beat:

2 eggs
1 cup apple juice or water
$\frac{1}{4}$ cup olive oil

Add:

$1\frac{1}{2}$ cups whole grain flour
$\frac{3}{4}$ cup buckwheat flour
$2\frac{1}{2}$ tsp. baking powder
$\frac{1}{2}$ tsp. salt

$\frac{1}{2}$ tsp. stevia
1 tsp. cinnamon
$\frac{1}{4}$ tsp. nutmeg
1 medium, peeled apple, chopped

Mix until just combined.
Fill greased muffin tin almost full. Bake 400° for 25 minutes.
                                        Yields 12 muffins

BLUEBERRY MUFFINS

Mix:

½ cup rolled oats	½ cup orange juice

Set aside.

Beat:

1 egg	½ cup olive oil

Add:

1½ cups whole grain flour	1 tsp. cinnamon
1½ tsp. baking powder	¼ tsp. nutmeg
¼ tsp. baking soda	1 tsp. stevia
½ tsp. cream of tartar	oats, orange juice mixture

Mix until just combined.

Fold in:
1 cup blueberries

Fill greased muffin tin almost full.
Bake 400° F. for 20 minutes.   Yields 12 muffins

DATE BRAN MUFFINS

In mixer bowl, beat:

2 eggs	1½ tsp. vanilla
¼ cup olive oil	

Add:

2 cups oat bran	1 tsp. stevia
2½ cups whole grain flour	1 tsp. cinnamon
2 tsp. baking powder	2 cups apple juice or water
1 tsp. baking soda	

Mix until just combined.

Fold in:

¾ cup chopped walnuts	1 cup chopped dates

Fill greased muffin tins almost full.
Bake 400° F. for 25 minutes.   Yields 2 dozen

Spiritual Nugget

First, talk to God about your children - then talk to your children about God.

15

HOLIDAY PECAN MUFFINS

In blender, process:

2 eggs

1 cup date pieces

Pour into mixer bowl and add:

1$\frac{1}{2}$ cups apple juice or water

$\frac{1}{4}$ cup olive oil

1 tsp. vanilla

Beat, then add:

3$\frac{1}{2}$ cups whole grain flour

2 Tbsp. baking powder

2 tsp. cream of tartar

1 tsp. stevia

$\frac{3}{4}$ tsp. salt

Mix until just combined.

Fold in:

1 cup chopped pecans

Fill greased muffin tin almost full. Bake 375° F. for 30 minutes.

Yields 18 muffins

JAM FILLED MUFFINS

Filling:

1 pint strawberry jam

Beat:

4 eggs

Add:

1$\frac{1}{3}$ cups milk or rice milk

$\frac{2}{3}$ cup apple sauce

3$\frac{1}{2}$ cups whole grain flour

2 Tbsp. baking powder

1 tsp. salt

1 tsp. stevia

Mix all ingredients and fill greased muffin tins half full.
Drop a spoonful of jam into center of batter.
Fill almost to the top of pan with remaining batter.
Bake 400° F. for 25 - 30 minutes or until golden brown.

Yields 24 muffins

ORANGE SPICE MUFFINS

In mixer bowl, beat:

1 egg

1/4 cup olive oil

1/2 cup apple sauce

1/4 cup orange juice concentrate

1 tsp. grated orange peel

Add:

1 1/2 cups whole grain flour

1/2 cup oat bran

1 1/2 tsp. baking powder

1/2 tsp. baking soda

1 tsp. stevia

1/2 tsp. cinnamon

1/4 tsp. ginger

1/8 tsp. cloves

Mix until just combined.
Spoon immediately into greased muffin tin.
Bake 375° F. for 25 minutes.

Delicious served warm with apple butter.   Yields 12 muffins

APPLE DATE BREAD

In mixer bowl, beat:

2 eggs

1 tsp. lemon juice

1/2 cup olive oil

1 tsp. vanilla

Add:

1 cup oat bran

3 1/2 cups whole grain flour

2 tsp. baking powder

1 1/2 tsp. baking soda

1 tsp. stevia, optional

2 Tbsp. cinnamon

1 tsp. nutmeg

1/2 tsp. ginger

1/2 tsp. allspice

1 3/4 cups apple juice or water

Tip:
Use sweet rather than tart apples in recipes. We prefer Yellow or Golden Delicious.

Mix until just combined.

Fold in:

1 1/2 cups finely shredded apples   1 cup date pieces

Spoon batter into two greased loaf pans.
Bake 350° F. for 60 minutes.   Yields 2 loaves

APPLE SAUCE BREAD

Soak in hot water:
1 cup raisins

Set aside.

Beat:

2 eggs	$^1/_2$ cup olive oil
1 cup apple sauce	1 tsp. vanilla

Add:

2 cups whole grain flour	$^3/_4$ tsp. salt
1 tsp. baking soda	2 tsp. cinnamon
1 tsp. baking powder	$^1/_2$ tsp. nutmeg
1$^1/_2$ tsp. stevia	

Add drained raisins and mix until just combined.
Pour into greased loaf pan.
Bake 350° F. for 1 hour.   Yields 1 loaf

Hint:
Apple sauce can be substituted for part or all of the butter in recipes.

APRICOT BANANA BREAD

In blender, process:

$^1/_4$ cup water	1 cup dried apricots

Set aside.

In mixing bowl, beat:

$^1/_3$ cup apple sauce	1 cup mashed ripe bananas
2 eggs	blended apricots

Add:

1$^3/_4$ cups whole grain flour	$^1/_2$ tsp. baking soda
$^1/_2$ cup oat bran	$^1/_2$ tsp. salt
1 tsp. stevia	$^1/_2$ cup chopped walnuts
1 tsp. baking powder	

Mix until just combined.
Pour into greased loaf pan.
Bake 350° F. for 1 hour.   Yields 1 loaf

BANANA BREAD

In mixer bowl, beat:
1/3 cup olive oil
2 eggs
1 1/2 cups mashed bananas

Add:
1 3/4 cups whole grain flour
1 tsp. baking soda
1 tsp. stevia
1/2 tsp. salt

Mix until just combined.

Fold in:
1/2 cup finely chopped nuts

Pour into greased loaf pan.
Bake 350° F. for 50 minutes.

Yields 1 loaf

Food for Thought:
Our attitudes are like ripples in water - they keep going out.

STRAWBERRY BREAD

In mixer bowl, beat:
3 eggs   1/2 cup olive oil

Add:
4 cups whole grain flour   1 tsp. ginger
1 1/2 tsp. stevia   1 tsp. salt
1 tsp. baking powder   3 cups sliced strawberries
1 tsp. baking soda   1/2 cup raisins
1/2 tsp. cream of tartar   1/2 cup chopped walnuts or pecans
2 tsp. cinnamon

Mix until just combined.
Divide batter between 2 greased loaf pans.
Bake 350° F. for 1 hour.   Yields 2 loaves

BANANA ORANGE BREAD

In mixer bowl, beat:
1½ cups ripe, mashed bananas
½ cup olive oil
3 eggs

Add:
3 cups whole grain flour
3 cups oat bran
5 tsp. baking powder
½ tsp. baking soda
1 tsp. stevia
1 Tbsp. finely grated orange peel

Mix until just combined.
Spread batter in two greased loaf pans.
Bake 350° F. for 45 minutes.

BLUEBERRY CORN BREAD

In mixing bowl, beat:
2 eggs
¼ cup apple sauce

Add:
1¼ cups cornmeal
1 cup whole grain flour
1 Tbsp. baking powder
½ tsp. stevia
⅔ cup apple juice or water

Mix until just combined.

Fold in:
½ cup blueberries

Pour into greased 8 x 8" baking pan.
Bake 425° F. for 25 minutes.
Cool before cutting.

*Food for
Thought:
Be patient with
the faults of
others; they
have to be
patient
with yours.*

CORN BREAD

In mixer bowl, beat:
1 egg
$^1/_3$ cup olive oil

Add:
1$^1/_2$ cups yellow cornmeal
1$^1/_2$ cups oat bran
1 Tbsp. baking powder
1 tsp. stevia
$^1/_4$ tsp. salt
1$^1/_2$ cups apple juice or water

Mix until just combined.
Pour into greased 8 x12" pan.
Bake 425° F. for 25 minutes.

CRANBERRY BREAD

In blender, chop:
1 - 12 oz. bag cranberries

Pour into mixer bowl and add:
3 eggs
$^1/_2$ cup olive oil
$^1/_4$ cup orange juice concentrate
1 Tbsp. grated orange peel
2 tsp. vanilla

Beat, then add:
3 cups whole grain flour
1 cup oat bran
1 Tbsp. baking powder
$^1/_2$ tsp. baking soda
1 Tbsp. cinnamon
$^1/_2$ tsp. cloves
1$^1/_2$ tsp. stevia
$^1/_4$ cup apple juice or water

Mix until just combined.
Divide into 2 greased loaf pans.
Bake 350° F. for 45 minutes.
Cool before slicing. Serve with apple butter.

Yields 2 loaves

PUMPKIN BREAD

In mixer bowl, beat:
2 cups canned pumpkin
3 eggs

$^1/_3$ cup apple sauce

Add:
3$^1/_3$ cups whole grain flour
1 tsp. baking powder
1$^1/_2$ tsp. baking soda
1$^1/_2$ tsp. cinnamon
$^1/_4$ tsp. ginger

$^1/_4$ tsp. cloves
1 tsp. stevia
$^1/_2$ tsp. salt
$^2/_3$ cup apple juice

Mix until just combined.

Fold in:
$^1/_2$ cup raisins, optional

Divide batter into 2 greased loaf pans.
Bake 350° F. for 1 hour and 15 minutes.
Cool slightly and remove from pans. Cool completely before slicing.

Butternut squash can be used in place of pumpkin in recipes calling for pumpkin.

CARROT ZUCCHINI BREAD

In blender, process until smooth:
$^1/_4$ cup apple sauce
$^3/_4$ cup prunes

1 cup water
1 tsp. vanilla

Pour into mixer bowl.

Add:
$^1/_2$ cup shredded zucchini
$^1/_2$ cup shredded carrots
3 cups whole grain flour
1 Tbsp. cinnamon

1$^1/_2$ tsp. baking soda
1 tsp. baking powder
1 tsp. stevia

Mix until just combined.
Spoon batter into a greased loaf pan.
Bake 350° F. for 1 hour.
Cool before slicing or it will fall apart.

ZUCCHINI BREAD

In mixer bowl, beat:

3 eggs
1/2 cup apple sauce
1/2 cup olive oil

1/2 cup orange juice
2 tsp. vanilla

Add:

2 3/4 cups whole grain flour
4 tsp. cinnamon
2 tsp. stevia

1 1/4 tsp. baking powder
1/2 tsp. baking soda
1 tsp. salt

Mix until just combined.

Fold in:

2 cups shredded zucchini

1 cup chopped pecans

Pour into 2 greased loaf pans.
Bake 350° F. for 1 hour.
Cool before slicing.

Yields 2 loaves

CINNAMON PECAN BREAD

Mix up 1 batch Whole Grain Bread dough. (page 26)
Cover and allow to rise for 1 hour.

In a small bowl, combine:

2 Tbsp. olive oil
1 tsp. stevia

2 tsp. cinnamon

Divide dough in half.
Roll each half out in a rectangle 14" x the length of your loaf pan.
Brush each rectangle with oil mixture.

Sprinkle over rectangle:

2 rounded Tbsp. finely chopped pecans

Beginning at short end, tightly roll dough up as for
jelly roll and shape into loaves.
Place in 2 greased loaf pans.
Sprinkle lightly with cinnamon.
Cover and allow to rise 30 - 40 minutes.
Bake 350° F. for 45 minutes.

Yields 2 loaves

FIBER
in the diet
protects against
colon cancer
and improves
digestion
of fats.

APRICOT BREAD

A delicious yeast bread!

In mixer bowl, combine:

1 1/2 cups orange juice, warm

2 Tbsp. yeast

1/4 cup white grape juice concentrate, warm

Let set until frothy.

Add:

1/4 cup olive oil

1/2 tsp. salt

1/2 tsp. baking soda

Add while mixing:

2 cups whole grain flour

Add:

1/2 cup chopped dried apricots

1/2 cup chopped pecans

While mixing, gradually add additional:

3 cups whole grain flour

Place in 2 greased loaf pans.
Cover and allow to rise in a warm place for 1 hour.
Bake 350° F. for 40 minutes.
Remove from pans. Cool completely before slicing or it falls apart.

Yields 2 loaves

Food for Thought: Nothing else ruins the truth like stretching it.

HERB BREAD

Mix up 1 batch Whole Grain Bread dough. (page 26)
Cover and allow to rise for 1 hour.

In a small bowl, combine filling:

2 Tbsp. olive oil

2 Tbsp. finely snipped chives

1 tsp. dill

1/4 tsp. garlic powder

Divide dough in half.
Roll each half out in a rectangle 14" x the length of your loaf pan.
Brush filling over each rectangle.
Beginning at short end, tightly roll dough up as for jelly roll and shape into loaves.
Place in 2 greased loaf pans. Cover and allow to rise 30 - 40 minutes.
Bake 350° F. for 45 minutes.

Yields 2 loaves

RYE BREAD STICKS

In mixer bowl, let set for 5 minutes:

1 cup warm water
1/4 cup white grape juice concentrate, warm

1 Tbsp. yeast

Add:

1/2 tsp. salt
3 Tbsp. olive oil

2 cups rye flour
1/2 tsp. stevia

While mixing with dough hooks or heavy mixer, slowly add:

2 - 2 1/2 cups whole grain flour

Cover and allow to rest 1 1/2 - 2 hours.
Divide dough into fourths, then divide each fourth into six pieces.
Roll each piece into a 9 inch rope. Fold in half and twist.
Place on baking sheet. Cover and allow to rise for 1 hour.
Gently brush beaten egg white over top.
Sprinkle sesame seeds over top.
Bake 400° F. for 20 minutes.

Yields 24 bread sticks

PUMPERNICKEL BREAD

A heavy tasty bread.

Combine and let set 10 minutes:

1/4 cup lukewarm white grape juice concentrate
1 1/2 cups lukewarm water

1 Tbsp. dry yeast

Food for Thought: A rumor is about as hard to unspread as butter.

Add:

1 1/2 tsp. salt
2 cups mashed potatoes, room temperature

2 Tbsp. olive oil
1/2 cup corn meal

Mix well.

While mixing, slowly add:

4 1/2 cups rye flour
3 1/2 cups whole grain flour

2 tsp. caraway seeds, optional

Cover and allow to rise in a warm place for 1 1/2 hours.
Work into 3 loaves. Place in greased pans.
Cover and allow to rise again for 1/2 - 1 hour.
Bake 350° F. for 1 hour.

Yields 3 loaves

WHOLE GRAIN BREAD

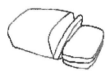

In mixer bowl, let set 10 minutes:
2 cups lukewarm water
1 Tbsp. yeast

¼ cup lukewarm white grape juice
concentrate

Add and mix:
2 Tbsp. olive oil
2 tsp. salt

2 cups whole grain flour

Continue mixing and slowly add:
6 cups whole grain flour

A little more flour may be needed if dough feels sticky.
Do not knead spelt bread any longer than needed to combine ingredients.
Kamut and wheat bread should be kneaded until smooth and elastic.
Cover with a towel in a warm place. Allow to rise for 1 hour or until double.
(I heat oven to about 90° F., turn it off and place bowl in oven.)
Work out into two loaves. Place in well greased loaf pans.
Prick all the way through in various places with fork.
Preheat oven to 325° F. Cover and allow to rise ½ hour on top of stove.
Bake 325° F. for 40 minutes.
When partially cool, remove from pans. Oil or butter tops.
Cover with a towel until cool. Slice.   Yields 2 loaves

HAMBURGER BUNS

Butter or Margarine?
Butter is preferable to margarine, but not too frequently. Totally avoid margarine.

Mix up one batch Whole Grain Bread dough.
Cover and allow to rise for 1 hour.
Punch down and divide in half.
Divide each half in ten pieces.
Roll each piece into a ball.
Flatten slightly on a greased cookie sheet.
Place at least one inch apart.
Brush tops with beaten egg white.
Sprinkle with sesame seeds.
Cover and allow to rise in a warm place for 30 minutes.
Bake 375° F. for 15 - 20 minutes.
Slice each bun in half.   Yields 20 hamburger buns

Main Dishes

ASPARAGUS AND CHICKEN

Place in 9 x 13" baking dish:
1½ lb. fresh asparagus, cut into 1 inch pieces.

In skillet, brown in 2 Tbsp. olive oil:
2 - 3 lb. skinless chicken breasts

(If pieces are thick, slice in half for a thinner breast)

Season with:
½ tsp. salt   ⅛ tsp. pepper

Arrange chicken on top of asparagus.

Bring to boil:
1½ cups chicken broth

While stirring constantly, pour in:
4 Tbsp. flour in ½ cup water

Continue stirring and boil for 2 minutes. Remove from heat.

Add:
½ cup mayonnaise   ¼ tsp. curry powder
2 tsp. lemon juice

Pour over chicken.
Cover and bake 375° F. for 1 hour or until
chicken is tender and juices run clear.   Serves 8 - 10

Tip:
Do not drain and rinse whole grain pasta for hot dishes. Just add your ingredients and serve.

PASTA AND ASPARAGUS

Cook:
½ lb. whole grain elbow macaroni according to directions

In skillet, saute in 2 Tbsp. olive oil:
1 garlic clove, minced
1 Tbsp. diced, hot pepper or green bell pepper
½ - 1 lb. fresh asparagus, cut into 1" pieces
1 tomato, chopped
¾ tsp. salt
⅛ tsp. pepper

Stir into macaroni and serve.   Serves 8

BLACK BEANS AND CORN BREAD

In skillet, saute in 1 Tbsp. olive oil:
1 onion, chopped
1 garlic clove, minced
1 bell pepper, diced
1 stalk celery, diced
1 carrot, finely chopped

Add:
2 cups black beans, drained
2 cups chunk tomatoes
$^1/_2$ tsp. oregano

Simmer uncovered for 10 minutes.
Pour into 8 x 8" greased baking pan.

CORN BREAD TOPPING

In mixing bowl, combine:
1 cup cornmeal
$^1/_3$ cup whole grain flour
$^1/_2$ tsp. baking powder
$^1/_4$ tsp. baking soda
$^1/_4$ tsp. cream of tartar
$^1/_2$ tsp. salt
$^1/_2$ cup corn

Add:
1 cup water
1 Tbsp. olive oil

Mix until just combined.
Pour over bean mixture.
Bake 400° F. for 35 minutes.

Tip:
If you have a food processor, chop extra onions and store in refrigerator up to a week, or freeze in small plastic bags or saran.

Serves 9

BROCCOLI RICE CASSEROLE

In large skillet, saute in 1 Tbsp. olive oil:
2 cups chopped, fresh or frozen broccoli, thawed
1 stalk celery, chopped
1 small onion, chopped
$^1/_2$ cup chopped, fresh mushrooms

Stir in:
2 Tbsp. whole grain flour   1 tsp. salt
2 cups chicken or turkey broth

Continue stirring.
Bring to a boil and continue boiling and stirring for 1 minute.

In casserole dish, place:
4 cups cooked brown rice

Pour vegetables over top. Don't stir.
Bake covered 325° F. for 30 minutes or until heated through.
If refrigerated, bake for 1 hour.   Serves 10 - 12

BEEF STEW

In heavy soup kettle, brown in 2 Tbsp. olive oil:
1 lb. chunk beef, cut in small bite sized pieces

Cover meat with water just to top of meat.
Simmer covered for 3 hours.

Add:
8 medium potatoes, bite sized chunks   1 medium onion, chopped
3 medium carrots, sliced $^1/_2$ tsp. salt
1 stalk celery, diced

Simmer covered for $^1/_2$ hour or until vegetables are tender.
Remove meat and vegetables from broth with a slotted spoon.
Place in serving bowl.

For gravy combine:
$^1/_2$ cup water   6 Tbsp. whole grain flour

Stir flour and water into boiling broth.
Continue stirring and boil for 2 minutes.
Add salt and pepper to taste.   Serves 8 - 10

*Food for
Thought:
Kindness is the
oil that takes the
friction out
of life.*

MEATBALL STEW

In a bowl, combine:

2 lb. ground beef
2 eggs
1 cup bread crumbs
2 Tbsp. onion, chopped

1 garlic clove, minced
1 tsp. salt
$\frac{1}{8}$ tsp. black pepper

Form into meat balls and brown in olive oil in large kettle.
Remove meat balls.

Add to kettle:

1 onion, sliced and separated
$1\frac{1}{3}$ cups water
4 medium carrots, chunked

8 medium potatoes, chunked
1 tsp. salt

Place meat balls on top.
Simmer covered for 30 minutes or until vegetables are tender.
Garnish with 2 Tbsp. parsley.

Note:

Can be done in 5 quart crock-pot, or $\frac{1}{2}$ batch in $3\frac{1}{2}$ quart crock-pot.
Brown meatballs in skillet. Place raw vegetables and meatballs in crock-pot.
Cook 8 hours on low, or 5 - 6 hours on high.   Serves 8 - 10

Food for Thought: Worry is like a rocking chair - it gives you something to do, but it doesn't get you any- where.

SAVORY BEEF STEW

In large skillet, brown for five minutes in 2 Tbsp. olive oil, turning often:
1 lb. bite sized, canned chunk beef or venison

Add:
1 medium onion, chopped

Cook for a few minutes.

Add:
1 cup water
5 medium potatoes, diced
2 cups frozen, mixed vegetables or your own combination, partially thawed

Cover and simmer for 45 minutes.

Stir $\frac{1}{4}$ cup whole grain flour and 1 tsp. salt into $\frac{1}{2}$ cup water.
Pour into stew, stirring constantly.
Continue cooking and stirring for 2 minutes after bubbly.   Serves 8

CHICKEN AND BEANS

Bring to a boil:
2 cups chicken broth

Dissolve:
2 Tbsp. cornstarch in ½ cup water

Stir into boiling broth.

Add:
2 cups cooked navy beans   2 cups cooked chicken pieces
2 cups cooked kidney beans

Heat.

In hot skillet, saute in 2 Tbsp. olive oil:
2 large carrots, thinly sliced   1 medium onion, diced
1 small garlic clove, minced

Add to bean mixture.

Add:
1 tsp. salt   dash cayenne pepper
½ tsp. ginger

Serve over cooked rice.   Serves 8

CHICKEN A LA KING

In skillet, bring to a boil:
2 cups chicken broth

Stir together:
1 cup milk or rice milk   ⅓ cup whole grain flour

Stir milk into boiling broth, stirring constantly.
Stir until thickened and bubbly.

Add:
2 cups cooked, chopped chicken   ⅛ tsp. ginger
1 Tbsp. minced onion   ½ tsp. salt
¼ tsp. paprika   pinch pepper
⅛ tsp. cayenne pepper   1 - 4 oz. can mushrooms

Heat.
Serve over biscuits or toast.   Serves 6

CHICKEN ASPARAGUS BISCUIT BAKE

In skillet, saute in 2 Tbsp. olive oil for about 10 minutes:
1 cup diced carrots
1 onion, chopped

Stir in:
2 cups cooked, chopped chicken
2 Tbsp. whole grain flour
1 1/2 cups chicken broth

Remove from heat when bubbly.

Add:
1 1/2 cups frozen, chopped asparagus, thawed
1 tsp. lemon juice
3/4 tsp. salt
1/8 tsp. pepper

Pour into 2 quart casserole.
Set aside.

BISCUITS

In mixer bowl, combine:
2 cups whole grain flour
4 tsp. baking powder
1 tsp. cream of tartar
1/4 tsp. garlic powder
1/8 tsp. salt
1/4 cup olive oil

Add:
7/8 cup water

Mix just until flour disappears.
Immediately, pour over casserole.
Bake uncovered 375° F. for 35 minutes.

Food for Thought:
Only the person who isn't rowing has time to rock the boat.

Serves 6

STUFFED CABBAGE ROLLS

In large kettle, bring water to a boil and add:
8 large cabbage leaves

Boil for 5 minutes.
Remove and rinse under cold water. Set aside.

STUFFING

Saute in 1 Tbsp. olive oil:
1/2 cup finely chopped celery   1 garlic clove, minced
1/4 cup finely chopped onion

Remove from heat and add:
3 cups cooked, flaked fish   1 Tbsp. lemon juice
2 cups cooked brown rice   1 tsp. salt
1 egg, slightly beaten   1/2 tsp. paprika
2 Tbsp. snipped fresh parsley   1/8 tsp. pepper

Mix well. Remove hard center rib from each cabbage leaf.
Place rounded 1/3 cup stuffing on each cabbage leaf.
Wrap up, tucking edges under. Place in 9 x 13" pan.
Top with ketchup. Cover and bake 350° F. for 45 minutes.

Serves 8

ROYAL DUMPLINGS

(Quick and easy)

Spiritual
Nugget:
Live so you're
neither afraid of
tomorrow, nor
ashamed of
yesterday.

In large skillet, combine:
1 cup cooked chicken, chopped   1 1/2 cups chicken or turkey broth
2 cups mixed frozen vegetables   1/4 tsp. salt

Cover and bring to a boil.

DUMPLINGS

Combine:
1 1/2 cups whole grain flour   1/2 tsp. salt
1 Tbsp. baking powder

Stir in with a fork until just moistened:
3/4 cup water

With a spoon, drop walnut size balls of dough into skillet in single layer.
Cover and simmer for 10 minutes.
Turn burner off and let set for 5 minutes.

Serves 7

RICE STUFFED CORNISH HEN

With rice as a side dish
(Pictured on front cover)

Allow 90 minutes baking time.
Determine how many cornish hens you need.
One cornish hen serves 2 people.

In kettle, simmer covered for about 45 minutes:
4 cups chicken broth
2$\frac{1}{2}$ cups water
1$\frac{1}{2}$ tsp. salt
1 cup uncooked brown rice
$\frac{3}{4}$ cup uncooked wild rice

In skillet, saute in 1 Tbsp. olive oil until almost tender:
1 cup chopped celery
$\frac{3}{4}$ cup chopped onion
1 cup fresh mushrooms, sliced

Add:
1 cup whole grain bread crumbs
1 tsp. thyme

Saute for 2 minutes.
Remove from heat and add cooked rice.
Spoon about $\frac{3}{4}$ cup stuffing into each cornish hen.
Place remaining rice in casserole. Extra broth will absorb during baking.
Cover and set aside.
Tie drum sticks together with string.
Bake breast side up, uncovered 375° F. for 40 minutes.

Meanwhile, pour in blender:
1 cup water
1 cup dried apricots
$\frac{1}{4}$ tsp. stevia

Process until smooth. Set aside.

Spread apricot sauce over hens and cover. Return to oven.
Bake 40 minutes longer or until done.
Also, put rice casserole in oven at this time.   Rice serves 10 - 12

DRESSING
(Good at Thanksgiving or anytime)

Saute in 2 Tbsp. olive oil about 5 minutes:
1 medium onion, finely chopped
2 stalks celery, chopped

1 medium carrot, finely chopped

Remove from heat.

Add:
1 tsp. salt
1/2 tsp. sage
1/4 tsp. thyme

1/4 tsp. rosemary
1/8 tsp. pepper

In a bowl, combine:
1/4 cup chopped fresh parsley
8 cups toasted whole grain bread,
              cut in 1/2" cubes

2 cups turkey or chicken broth
sautéed vegetables

Pour into greased 9 x 13" pan. Cover with foil.
Bake 350° F. for 45 minutes.
Remove foil halfway through baking time.   Serves 10 - 12

Note:
Also delicious for stuffing a turkey. Use 1/4 cup less broth.
Bake according to turkey directions, adding 1/2 hour.

QUICK STOVETOP STUFFING

In skillet, saute in 3 Tbsp. olive oil:
1 onion, diced

1 stalk celery, finely chopped

Add:
1 tsp. marjoram
1/2 tsp. sage
1/2 tsp. thyme

1/2 tsp. salt
1/4 tsp. pepper

Stir, then add:
4 cups whole grain bread crumbs

Stir until well coated.

Add:
1/2 cup broth or water

Continue cooking and stirring for 5 - 6 minutes.

Note:
To stuff a turkey, omit 5 - 6 minutes cooking time.

ITALIAN STUFFED EGGPLANT

1 large eggplant

Cut eggplant in half lengthwise.
With a paring knife, cut around the edge, leaving ¼" thick shell.
Scoop out pulp and chop.
Set aside.
Place shells in baking dish.

Brown in large skillet:
½ lb. ground beef

Add:
1 medium onion, chopped
1 garlic clove, minced
2 Tbsp. chopped green bell pepper
2 cups chopped tomatoes
chopped eggplant pulp

Continue cooking for 10 minutes, stirring often.

Add:
½ tsp. oregano
¼ tsp. thyme
¼ tsp. basll
½ tsp. salt
⅛ tsp. pepper
1 slice whole grain bread, crumbled

Fill eggplant shells.
Cover and bake 350° F. for 45 minutes.
Sprinkle cheese over top and bake another
5 minutes or until cheese is melted.

Serves 4 - 6

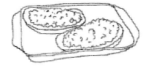

ENCHILADAS

In skillet, saute in 1 Tbsp. olive oil:
1 onion, chopped   1 Tbsp. chopped bell pepper

Add and combine:
2 cups cooked, chopped chicken   1/2 tsp salt
1/4 cup whole grain flour

While stirring constantly, slowly add:
1 cup broth

Bring to a boil and continue stirring for 2 minutes.
Remove from heat.

Heat 18 - 5" tortillas until warm and flexible.
Spread a thin layer of salsa on bottom of 9 x 13" baking pan.
Place 1 1/2 Tbsp. filling on tortilla, slightly to one side.
Roll up and place seam side down in pan.
Spread salsa over top.
Bake covered 350° F. for 25 minutes or until hot.   Serves 6

TURKEY BEAN ENCHILADAS

In skillet, saute in 1 Tbsp. olive oil:
2 cups cooked, chopped turkey   1 garlic clove, minced
1 onion, chopped

Stir in:
2 cups cooked kidney beans   1/8 tsp salt
1 1/4 cups pizza sauce

Cook covered over low heat for 10 minutes.
Heat 18 - 5" corn tortillas until warm and flexible.
Spread a thin layer of salsa on bottom of 9 x 13" baking pan.
Spoon 3 Tbsp. of the mixture onto each tortilla.
Roll up and place seam side down in pan.
Spread salsa over top.
Cover and bake 375° F. for 20 minutes.   Serves 6 - 8

CORN TORTILLAS

In mixer bowl, beat:
2 eggs
1 cup cornmeal
2 cups whole grain flour
1 tsp. baking powder
1/2 tsp. salt
3 cups cold water

Pour 1/4 cup of batter at a time onto greased hot griddle or heavy skillet,
spreading to 5 inch circle.
Stir batter each time.
Turn when tortilla looks dry. Lightly brown second side.
Remove and keep warm.   Yields 18 tortillas

Note:
For soft tacos, warm tortillas. Have each person put his own toppings on, and roll up to eat.

FLOUR TORTILLAS

Beat:
3 eggs

Add:
1 1/2 cups whole grain flour
1 cup milk or rice milk
1/2 tsp. salt

In greased skillet, over medium heat, drop 2 Tbsp. batter.
Immediately, spread to 5 inch circle.
Cook uncovered until set. Do not brown or turn.
Remove from skillet and set aside.   Yields 18 tortillas

Note:
Can be made ahead and refrigerated.

To warm, wrap tortillas in a tea towel:
In crockpot, stagger all of the tortillas, heat on warm for 1/2 hour. (or)
In microwave, stack 9 at a time. Heat for 1/2 - 1 minute on high.

ENCHILADA CASSEROLE

Brown:
1 lb. ground turkey or beef

Add:
1 onion, chopped

1 garlic clove, minced

Cook until tender.

Add:
1 quart pizza sauce
1 tsp. salt
1/8 tsp. pepper

1/2 tsp. oregano
1/4 tsp. thyme

Stir together and heat.

Cut 9 flour tortillas (page 39) in half.
Place around outside of 8 x 12" pan on bottom, as shown in diagram.
Place a whole tortilla in the middle. Spread with 1/3 of the meat mixture.
Repeat layers 2 times, ending with meat on top.
Bake uncovered 375° F. for 20 minutes.   Serves 7

VEGETABLE FISH BAKE

Place in bottom of 8 x 8" baking pan:
1 lb fish, cooked

Layer over fish:
2 cups thinly sliced zucchini
1 cup thinly sliced carrots

Combine:
3 Tbsp. lemon juice
1 Tbsp. chopped parsley
1 tsp. fresh dill
1/2 tsp salt
1/8 tsp. pepper

Sprinkle over vegetables.
Cover and bake 425° F. for 30 minutes.   Serves 6

TUNA TORTILLA BAKE

In skillet, stir together:

1/4 cup olive oil

1/2 cup whole grain flour

Stir until bubbly.
Remove from heat.

Slowly add, while stirring:
2 cups milk or rice milk

Return to heat.
Continue stirring until thickened.

Add:

1/2 tsp. paprika

1/2 tsp. salt

1/4 tsp. pepper

2 - 6 oz. cans tuna, drained

1 Tbsp. diced onion

1 cup fresh chopped mushrooms

1 Tbsp. parsley

Spread over bottom of 9 x 13" baking pan:
1 cup pizza sauce

Fill Flour Tortillas (page 39) with 3 Tbsp. filling. Roll up and place in pan, seam side down.
Cover with 1 cup pizza sauce.
Bake covered 350° F. for 20 minutes.
Uncover and bake an additional 20 minutes.   Serves 6

FISH CREOLE

In large skillet, saute for 2 minutes in 2 Tbsp. olive oil:

1 stalk celery, thinly sliced

1 green pepper, chopped

2 Tbsp. chopped onion

Add:

4 cups peeled, chopped tomatoes

1 lb. fish filets, cut in 1" pieces

2 Tbsp. vinegar

1 tsp. salt

1/4 tsp. marjoram

1/8 tsp. cayenne pepper

dash garlic salt

Cook 15 minutes, occasionally stirring gently, or until fish flakes easily.
Serve over brown rice.   Serves 8

Oven cooked rice:
Pour 6 cups of water into a 2 1/2 quart casserole. Add 2 cups brown rice and 1 tsp. salt. Bake covered at 350 F. for 1 1/2 hours.

TUNA LASAGNE

Cook 6 whole grain lasagne noodles according to directions.

Tip:
Lasagne will not stick together as readily when cooking, if you add 1 Tbsp. of oil to the cooking water.

SAUCE

In sauce pan, heat:
$1/4$ cup olive oil

Stir into heated oil:
$1/2$ cup whole grain flour

Slowly add:
2 cups milk or water

Stir constantly until thickened.

Add:
$1/2$ tsp. salt
$1/4$ tsp. pepper

Set aside.

Combine:
1 egg, beaten, opt.
2 - 6 oz. cans tuna, drained
1 garlic clove, minced
1- 4 oz. can mushrooms
1 cup fresh tomatoes, chopped
$1/8$ tsp. cayenne pepper
1 Tbsp. fresh parsley, finely chopped

Stir into sauce.
In 8 x 12" pan, spread thin layer of sauce over bottom of pan.
Cover with 3 noodles.
Spread half of sauce over noodles.
Add 3 remaining noodles.
Spread with remaining sauce.
Top with 1 cup grated cheese.
Bake 350° F. for 30 minutes.

Serves 6 - 8

VEGETABLE LASAGNE

Cook:
8 whole grain lasagne noodles according to directions.

Brown:
½ lb. ground beef

Continue heating and add:
1 large onion, chopped
1 garlic clove, minced
1 stalk celery, chopped
1 medium carrot, shredded
¾ tsp. oregano
½ tsp. basil
¼ tsp. marjoram
¼ tsp. rosemary
½ tsp. salt
½ cup whole grain flour

While stirring constantly, add:
1 quart tomato juice

Simmer for 5 minutes, stirring occasionally.
Set aside.

Combine:
1 egg, beaten
1½ cups cooked, chopped spinach
8 oz. shredded mozzarella cheese

Food for Thought:
Every man should keep a fair sized cemetary in which to bury the faults of his friends.

In 9 x 13" pan, evenly spread a thin layer of meat sauce over the bottom.
Top with half of the noodles, (overlapping slightly if necessary) half of the cheese mixture, and half of the meat sauce.
Repeat layers, ending with meat sauce on top.
Bake covered at 350° F. for 1 hour.
Can be assembled, refrigerated, and baked the next day.   Serves 8

VEGETARIAN LASAGNE

Cook 6 lasagne noodles according to directions.

Saute in 2 Tbsp. olive oil:

1 stalk celery, diced   1 small onion, diced
1 garlic clove, minced

Add:

5 cups cooked kidney beans   1/2 tsp. basil
1 cup salsa   1/2 tsp. salt
1 Tbsp. parsley, snipped

Stir to combine. Remove from heat.
Place 3 lasagne noodles in greased 8 x 12" baking pan.
Spread 1/2 of the bean mixture over noodles.

Add:

3 more lasagne noodles and the rest of the beans.

Top with shredded cheese.
Bake 350° F. for 35 minutes.   Serves 6 - 8

MEAT CRUST PIE

Mix together in a bowl:

1 lb. ground beef   1/4 cup fine bread crumbs
1/2 cup mushroom soup (page 87)   2 Tbsp. chopped fresh parsley
1 egg, beaten   1/2 tsp. salt
1 onion, chopped   1/8 tsp. pepper

Press into bottom and sides of 9" pie pan.
Bake 350° F. for 25 minutes.
Drain grease off.

Meanwhile, whip together:

2 cups mashed potatoes   1 cup Mushroom Soup (page 87)

Spread over baked meat crust.

Optional:

Top with shredded cheese and/or Fakin Bacon Bits.

Bake 15 minutes or until heated through.   Serves 6

CHILI MAC CASSEROLE

Cook according to package directions:
1¹/₂ cups whole grain macaroni

Brown:
1 lb. ground beef   1 medium onion, chopped

Add:
1 quart tomato chunks or juice   1 tsp. chili powder
3 cups cooked kidney beans   ¹/₂ tsp. cumin
1 - 4.25 oz. can chopped olives   1¹/₂ tsp. salt
1 Tbsp. chopped hot peppers   ¹/₂ tsp. pepper
¹/₄ tsp. minced garlic   cooked macaroni

Bake uncovered in a 9 x 13" cake pan at 375° F. for 25 - 30 minutes.
Optional: Top with shredded cheese.
Bake another 5 - 8 minutes or until cheese is melted.   Serves 12

MACARONI CASSEROLE

When browning ground beef or turkey, brown as much as will fit in your skillet. Freeze the extra for quick meal preparation.

Cook according to directions:
10 oz whole grain macaroni

Brown:
¹/₂ lb. ground beef

Add:
1 onion, diced   dash garlic powder
1 Tbsp. diced green pepper   ¹/₂ tsp. salt
3 cups pizza sauce   ¹/₈ tsp. pepper
¹/₂ tsp. basil   1 - 4.25 oz. can chopped olives, undrained
¹/₂ tsp. oregano   1 pint corn

Add macaroni and pour into casserole.
Bake 350° F. for 1 hour.   Serves 8

EASY MACARONI CASSEROLE

Brown:
1/2 lb. ground beef or turkey

Add:
1 small onion, chopped
1 bell pepper, chopped
1 Tbsp. Taco Seasoning (page 176)
1/2 tsp. salt
2 cups pizza sauce
3/4 cup water
12 oz. whole grain macaroni, cooked according to directions

Pour into casserole.
Bake covered 350° F. for 35 minutes.

Serves 6

Tip:
Cover ground beef to brown it. You will be able to drain the fat off rather than frying it into the meat.

ITALIAN MACARONI

Brown:
1/2 lb. ground beef

Add:
1 medium onion, chopped
1 stalk celery, chopped

2 Tbsp. chopped green bell pepper

Cook until onion is clear.

Add and simmer 15 minutes:
1 quart tomato chunks
1 tsp. oregano
1/2 tsp. basil

1 tsp. salt
1/8 tsp. pepper

Cook according to package directions:
10 oz. whole grain elbow macaroni

Add macaroni to tomatoes.
Simmer 5 additional minutes.

Serves 6

SOUR CREAM FISH CASSEROLE

Cook:
4 large potatoes until just softened (about 30 minutes)

Sour cream mixture:
1½ cups sour cream and ½ cup water or 1½ cups yogurt
2 Tbsp. snipped chives
½ tsp. salt
⅛ tsp. pepper

In greased 9 x 13" pan, layer in order given:
cooled, thinly sliced potatoes
⅔ cup of the sour cream mixture
2 lbs. fish, cut in 1 inch pieces
1 medium onion, cut in rings
remainder of sour cream mixture
bell pepper strips, optional
2 Tbsp. snipped parsley

Bake uncovered 325° F. for 1 hour or until fish flakes easily.   Serves 8

Food for Thought:
The only persons you should want to get even with are those who have helped you.

SKILLET MEATLOAF DINNER

Mix together in a bowl:

1 lb. ground beef
¼ cup chicken or turkey broth
¾ cup whole grain flour
½ cup whole grain bread crumbs
½ cup chopped green peppers
2 Tbsp. ketchup

1 small onion, chopped
½ tsp. salt
⅛ tsp. cream of tartar
⅛ tsp. baking soda
⅛ tsp. pepper

Pat mixture into a 9 inch skillet to within 1 inch of the edge.

Pour around the edge:
½ cup chicken or turkey broth

Place on top of meat mixture in spoke fashion:
3 medium potatoes, cut in wedges

Lightly sprinkle salt over potatoes.
Simmer covered, over low heat until potatoes are tender. (about 40 minutes)
Garnish with chopped parsley if desired.   Serves 6

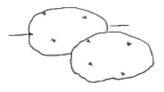

SAVORY SPLIT PEAS

In large skillet or soup kettle, saute in 1 Tbsp. olive oil:

1 onion, chopped   1 stalk celery, chopped
2 Tbsp. finely chopped red bell pepper

Add:

2 cups water   5 medium potatoes, cubed
2 cups chicken broth   1 tsp. salt
2 cups split peas

Simmer covered for 40 minutes.

Add:

1 tsp. thyme $^1/_8$ tsp. pepper
$^1/_2$ tsp. rosemary

Stir and serve.   Serves 10

STUFFED PEPPERS √

Arrange in baking pan:

4 large green peppers, seeded and cut in half lengthwise

In mixing bowl, combine:

1 lb. ground beef   2$^1/_2$ cups cooked brown rice
1 onion, chopped

Set aside.

SAUCE

In a measuring cup, combine:

$^3/_4$ cup pizza sauce or ketchup $^3/_4$ tsp. salt
1 Tbsp. vinegar $^1/_8$ tsp. pepper
1 tsp. mustard

Stir half of the sauce into the meat.
Reserve the rest for over top.
Spoon meat into pepper halves, dividing evenly.
Spread sauce over top.
Bake uncovered 350° F. for 1$^1/_2$ hours.

HOMEMADE NOODLES

Beat until very light:
4 eggs or 8 egg yolks

Add:
1/2 cup cold water   1/2 tsp. salt, optional
2 Tbsp. olive oil

Using dough hook, add 4 1/2 - 5 cups whole grain flour while mixing.
Dough should be stiff and not sticky.
Divide in 4 parts and work each part until smooth, adding more flour
if needed. Put through pasta maker.

> **Whole grain pasta** should be stored in the freezer.

PIZZA CRUST

In mixer bowl, combine:
3/4 cup warm water
2 Tbsp. white grape juice concentrate, warm
2 tsp. yeast

Let set for 5 minutes.

Add:
2 Tbsp. olive oil
2 1/2 cups whole grain flour, room temperature
1/2 tsp. garlic powder
1/2 tsp. basil
1/4 tsp. salt

Mix well. Place on greased pizza pan.
Allow to rise in warm place for 20 minutes.
Bake 400° F. for 12 minutes.
Add toppings and bake 350° F. for 20 minutes.

CHICKEN PIZZA

Spread over prebaked crust in order given:
2 cups cooked, chopped chicken   3 cups pizza sauce
1 red bell pepper, chopped   2 cups shredded cheese
1 Tbsp. minced onion

Bake 375° F. for 20 minutes or until cheese is melted.

FISH POT PIE

PASTRY

Combine:

$^1/_3$ cup olive oil

$2^1/_3$ cups whole grain flour

1 Tbsp. baking powder

pinch salt

Add:

$^1/_2$ cup milk or rice milk

Mix just until dough forms a ball. Don't over-mix.
Divide dough almost in half. Roll larger piece out on lightly floured counter.
Fold in half, then in half again. Place in 9" pie pan.
Unfold and press against bottom and sides of pan.
Trim dough around edge of pan.

FILLING

Heat in skillet over medium heat:

1 Tbsp. olive oil

Stir in:

2 Tbsp. whole grain flour

$^1/_2$ tsp. salt

$^1/_8$ tsp. pepper

dash garlic powder

While stirring, gradually add:

$^3/_4$ cup broth

Cook, stirring constantly, until thickened and bubbly, about 3 minutes.
Set aside.

In a bowl, combine:

2 cups potatoes, diced approx. $^1/_4$ inch pieces
1 cup flaked, cooked fish, drained (about $^3/_4$ lb. frozen)
$^1/_2$ cup sliced fresh mushrooms
$^1/_4$ cup thinly sliced carrots
$^1/_4$ cup peas
1 Tbsp. finely chopped onion

Stir thickened sauce into vegetables. Fill unbaked pie shell with mixture.
Roll out remaining dough. Place on top. Moisten edges, seal, and flute.
Cut slits in top. Brush top with egg white.
Bake 375° F. for 1 hour.
Let set 5 - 10 minutes before cutting.

POT PIE

Use pastry from Fish Pot Pie. (page 50)

FILLING

Brown:
1/2 lb. ground beef

Add:

1 onion, chopped
1 garlic clove, minced
1 tsp. salt
1/2 tsp. sage
1/2 tsp. thyme

1/4 tsp. allspice
1/8 tsp. pepper
1/8 tsp. cloves
2/3 cup ketchup

Stir well and add:

3 cooked potatoes, cubed

2 cooked carrots, diced

Fill unbaked pie shell with mixture. Roll out remaining dough. Place on top.
Moisten edges, seal, and flute. Cut slits in top. Brush top with egg white.
Bake 375° F. for 35 minutes. Allow to set for 10 minutes before cutting.

Spiritual
Nugget:
Work as if you'll
live to be 100. Pray
as if you'll die
tomorrow.

VEGETABLE POT PIE

In large skillet, saute for 5 minutes in 1 Tbsp. olive oil:

1 onion, chopped
1/2 cup chopped red bell peppers

1 garlic clove, minced

Add:

2 cups broth
1 large potato, cubed
2 small zucchini, sliced
1 carrot, diced
1/2 cup peas

1/2 cup corn
1/2 tsp. rosemary
1/4 tsp. thyme
3/4 tsp. salt
pepper to taste

Simmer covered for 5 minutes. Stir 3 Tbsp. whole grain flour into 1/3 cup water.
Add to vegetables, stirring constantly until bubbly. Pour into 2 quart casserole.

In mixer bowl, combine:

2 cups whole grain flour
4 tsp. baking powder
1 tsp. cream of tartar

1/4 tsp. garlic powder
1/8 tsp. salt
1/4 cup olive oil

Add:

7/8 cup water

Mix until just combined. Immediately spread over vegetables.
Bake uncovered 400° F. for 20 minutes.

Serves 8 - 10

STUFFED BAKED POTATOES

Bake uncovered 400° F. for 1½ hours:
6 large baking potatoes

FILLING

Saute in 1 Tbsp. olive oil until tender (about 10 minutes):
1 small onion, chopped
1 cup diced carrots
1 cup finely chopped broccoli
1 cup finely chopped cauliflower
¼ cup chopped bell pepper

Remove from heat.

Add:
2 - 6 oz. cans tuna
½ tsp. salt
⅛ tsp. pepper
2 Tbsp. olive oil
½ cup cheese, optional

Cut each potato in half when cool enough to handle.
Scoop pulp out, leaving a thin layer of potato on skin.
Mash pulp and stir filling in. Form filling with hands, pressing together.
Place in potato shells.
Bake covered 350° F. for 20 minutes.

Food for Thought: Worry pulls tomorrow's cloud over today's sunshine.

QUICK SUPPER CASSEROLE ✓

Combine in casserole:
3 cups sliced cooked potatoes
2 cups frozen peas
1 cup chopped, cooked chicken
2 cups Mushroom Soup (page 87)
½ tsp. salt

Bake covered 350° F. for 1 hour.

Serves 5

MEXICAN CORN AND RICE

Total baking time is 1 hour and 40 minutes.

In large skillet, saute for 6 - 8 minutes in 1 Tbsp. olive oil:
1½ cups uncooked brown rice   1 Tbsp. diced green pepper
1 small onion, minced   1 small garlic clove, minced

Transfer to large casserole.

Add:
¾ tsp. salt   3 cups tomato juice
1 tsp. chili powder   1½ cups water
¼ tsp. cumin

Bake covered 350° F. for 1 hour.

Add:
1 pint corn, thawed

Cover and bake for 40 minutes longer.   Serves 10 - 12

FRIED RICE

In a large skillet, saute in 2 Tbsp. olive oil for 3 minutes:
1 cup chopped carrots
1 chopped onion
1 garlic clove, minced

Add and saute 4 minutes:
1 cup uncooked brown rice

Add and simmer covered for 40 minutes:
2½ cups chicken broth
1 tsp. salt

Add and simmer for 10 more minutes:
¾ cup frozen peas

Serve immediately.
If reheating, add a little water.   Serves 8

Tip:
White rice has the brownish outer skin removed, taking away the fiber and minerals. Brown rice is nutritious, but gets rancid quickly. Store in the refrigerator.

VEGGIE RICE CASSEROLE

In soup kettle, simmer covered, for 1 hour:

1 cup uncooked brown rice	1 tsp. salt
4 cups chicken broth	$1/8$ tsp. curry powder

Add:

1 cup mixed vegetables or any kind of leftover vegetables

Heat and serve.

Note:

Can be combined in 2 quart casserole.
Bake 350° F. for $1^1/_2$ hours.
Add vegetables, thawed, last 15 minutes.   Serves 6

DELUXE CHICKEN AND RICE

With a sharp knife or kitchen shears, cut:

$^3/_4$ - 1 lb. chicken breasts in 1 inch cubes

In large skillet, combine:

$4^1/_2$ cups water	chicken

Bring to a boil and simmer covered, for $1/2$ hour.
(Stir the chicken apart if stuck together.)

Add:

$1^1/_2$ cups uncooked brown rice	1 Tbsp. chopped red bell pepper
1 medium carrot, diced	$1^1/_2$ tsp. salt

Bring to a boil again and simmer covered for 1 hour.

Add:

1 tsp. chili powder	$1/8$ tsp. garlic powder
$1/2$ tsp. cumin	$1/8$ tsp. pepper
$1/4$ tsp. turmeric	

Stir together and serve.   Serves 6 - 8

Food for Thought:

Instead of pointing a critical finger, try holding out a helping hand.

ORIENTAL FRIED RICE

In large kettle, saute for 5 minutes in 2 Tbsp. olive oil:
2 carrots, diced
2 stalks celery, diced
1 onion, chopped

1 garlic clove
2 cups uncooked brown rice

Add and saute 2 minutes longer:
5 large, fresh mushrooms, sliced
2 cups snowpeas, bite size

2 cups chopped cabbage

Add:
4 cups chicken broth
2 cups water

2 tsp. salt
$1/4$ tsp. pepper

Simmer covered for 45 minutes or until rice is done.   Serves 10

Food for Thought: Habits are like a soft bed... it's easy to get in, but hard to get out.

ORIENTAL SKILLET DINNER

Bring to a boil in kettle:
6 cups water
2 cups uncooked brown rice

1 tsp. salt

Simmer covered for 1 hour.

In large skillet, brown:
$1/2$ lb. ground beef

Add and continue cooking for 2 minutes:
1 onion, chopped
1 garlic clove, minced

2 stalks celery, sliced crosswise

Add:
4 cups tomato chunks or juice
6 cups chopped cabbage
2 tsp. chili powder

$1/2$ tsp. ginger
1 tsp. salt
$1/8$ tsp. pepper

Cover and allow to simmer for 20 minutes.
Serve over brown rice.   Serves 10

CROCK-POT ROAST

In crock-pot, place in order given:

3 cups bite size carrot chunks
6 medium potatoes, quartered
1 large onion, sliced and
　　　　　　separated into rings

1 stalk celery, diced
1 cup water

Salt and pepper both sides:
2 lbs. rump or chuck roast

Place on top of vegetables.

Drizzle over meat:
1 Tbsp. lemon juice

Cover and cook on low for 9 - 10 hours.　　　　Serves 6 - 7

SALMON PILAF

In sauce pan, saute in 1 Tbsp. olive oil until tender:
1 medium onion, chopped　　　　1 garlic clove, minced

Add and saute for 2 minutes:
1 cup uncooked brown rice

Add:
$3/4$ tsp. salt
$1/4$ tsp. turmeric
dash pepper

2 cups chicken or turkey broth
1 cup water

Simmer covered for $1/2$ hour.

Add:
2 - 6 oz. cans salmon, drained

Simmer covered for 15 more minutes.

Just before serving, add:
2 Tbsp. chopped fresh parsley, optional　　　　Serves 4

SPAGHETTI

Saute in 1 Tbsp. olive oil:

1 cup finely chopped carrots
1 stalk celery, chopped
1 garlic clove, minced

1 onion, chopped
1/2 cup chopped green pepper

Add:

1 quart tomato juice
1/2 lb. ground beef, browned
1 - 4 oz. can mushrooms, drained
1 - 4 1/4 oz. can chopped olives, drained

1 tsp. oregano
1/2 tsp. paprika
1 tsp. salt

Simmer covered for 20 minutes.

Add:

10 oz. whole grain spaghetti, cooked according to directions.

Heat and serve.   Serves 8

To save on food preparation time later, make a double batch and refrigerate for use in a few days or freeze.

CHICKEN SPAGHETTI

Cook according to directions:

10 oz. whole grain spaghetti

In a large skillet, saute in 1 Tbsp. olive oil:

1 small onion, diced
1 clove garlic, minced
1/2 cup chopped, fresh mushrooms or 1 - 4 oz. can, drained

Add:

1 quart tomato chunks
2 cups chopped, cooked chicken
2 Tbsp. vinegar

1 tsp. paprika
1/2 tsp. basil
1/2 tsp. salt

Simmer uncovered for 1/2 hour, stirring occasionally.
Add spaghetti and mix together.   Serves 8 - 10

SPAGHETTI AND MEATBALLS

Cook:
10 oz. whole grain spaghetti according to directions

Drain.

Add:
1 quart pizza sauce
1 Tbsp. parsley
1 tsp. Italian Seasoning
1/2 tsp. basil
1/2 tsp. oregano
dash garlic powder
1 tsp. salt
dash pepper

Stir well and heat.
Add meatballs to serve.

MEATBALLS

In bowl, combine:
1 lb. ground beef or turkey
1 egg
1 Tbsp. onion
1/2 cup bread crumbs
1/2 tsp. Italian Seasoning
1/8 tsp. oregano
1/8 tsp. basil
1/2 tsp. salt
1/8 tsp. pepper

Food for Thought:
Our duty is not to see through one another, but to see one another through.

Form into 1 - 1 1/2 inch meat balls.
Place on baking pan.
Bake uncovered 375° F. for 30 minutes.

Serves 6

SPAGHETTI SQUASH

Cut 1 large spaghetti squash in half. Scrape seeds out.
Place cut side down in skillet with $1/2$ - 1 cup water.
Cover and cook for $1/2$ hour or until just tender.
Rake spaghetti out with fork and add to sauce.

SAUCE

Saute in 1 Tbsp. olive oil:
1 medium onion, chopped   1 garlic clove, minced

Add:
3 cups tomato chunks   1 tsp. salt
1 tsp. basil $1/8$ tsp. pepper
1 tsp. oregano

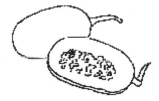

Remove from heat.

Add:
1 cup whole grain bread crumbs
$1/2$ lb. ground beef, browned or meat balls, optional

Combine with spaghetti squash, and pour into casserole.
Bake covered 375° F. for 35 minutes.   Serves 6 - 8

VEGGIE WILD RICE SKILLET

In a large skillet, saute for 5 minutes in 2 Tbsp. olive oil:
$2/3$ cup uncooked brown rice
$1/3$ cup uncooked wild rice

Add:
$3^{1}/2$ cups chicken broth
1 tsp. salt
dash pepper

Simmer covered for $1/2$ hour.

Add:
2 cups mixed vegetables

Simmer covered for $1/2$ hour longer or until done.   Serves 6 - 8

*Food for
Thought:
When you spill
anger, it can't
be mopped
up.*

VEGGIE STIR-FRY
Delicious served over rice.

Prepare all vegetables before heating skillet.

In large heavy skillet, stir fry in 2 Tbsp. olive oil:

2 cups sliced carrots
1 cup broccoli florets
2 cups cauliflower florets
2 cups snow peas

1 cup sliced fresh mushrooms
3 cups shredded cabbage
1 onion, sliced and separated into rings
1 stalk celery, chopped

Cook, stirring frequently until tender-crisp.

Meanwhile, stir together:

1 cup broth
1½ tsp. salt

1 Tbsp. lemon juice
2 Tbsp. cornstarch

Stir into vegetables. Continue stirring until thickened.
Serve over brown rice.

Serves 10

SWEET POTATO BEAN CASSEROLE

Saute in 1 Tbsp. olive oil for 4 minutes:
1 onion, chopped
1 garlic clove, minced

Add and saute for 2 minutes:
⅓ cup uncooked brown rice

Add:
1½ cups chopped tomatoes
2 cups cooked great northern or navy beans
2 Tbsp. chopped red bell pepper
2 medium sweet potatoes, shoe stringed
1 cup water
½ tsp. salt

Bring to a boil.
Cover and simmer 50 minutes or until rice is tender.

Serves 8

TACO CASSEROLE

In skillet, saute in 1 Tbsp. olive oil:
1 medium onion, chopped
1 garlic clove, minced
1 cup chopped fresh mushrooms
1 Tbsp. chopped green bell pepper

In blender, process:
4 cups kidney beans, drained
2 cups tomato juice

Pour in skillet.

Add:
1 Tbsp. finely chopped hot pepper
2 tsp. chili powder
$1/2$ tsp. cumin
$1/4$ tsp. celery seed
$1/2$ tsp. salt
$1/8$ tsp. pepper

Simmer for 5 minutes.

Break up into bite size pieces:
1 - 11 oz. bag tortilla chips

In 8 x 12" baking pan, spread out half of the chips.
Spread bean mixture evenly over chips.
Spread a thin layer of sour cream or yogurt over if desired.
Sprinkle the rest of the chips over top.

Sprinkle over top:
$1^1/2$ cups cheddar cheese

Bake 300° F. for 5 minutes or until cheese is melted.

Sprinkle over top and serve immediately:
1 large tomato, chopped
$1^1/2$ cups finely chopped lettuce   Serves 8

Spiritual Nugget:
Feed your faith, and your doubts will starve to death.

TACO DIP

Serve with tortilla chips.

Brown:
1 lb. ground beef

Add and cook until clear:
1 medium onion, chopped

Add:

2 tsp. chili powder

1 tsp. paprika

1/2 tsp. cumin

1/2 tsp. salt

2 Tbsp. whole grain flour

1 cup tomato juice

Cook for 10 minutes, stirring occasionally.

Blend:
2 1/2 cups kidney beans, undrained
1/4 tsp. salt

Add water if too thick to blend.

Layer in 9 x 13" pan in order given:
hamburger
beans

Heat in 350° F. oven for 5 minutes.

Continue layers:
sour cream or yogurt
chopped lettuce
shredded cheese
chopped tomatoes

Put in oven just until cheese melts.

To serve:
Spoon onto your plate, and dip chips in to eat.

Note:
You can prepare meat and beans ahead of time and refrigerate.
Spread on pan and warm in oven about 20 minutes.
Add the rest of the toppings.   Serves 8 -10 people

TACO PIE

Combine:
1 lb. ground beef, browned
1 onion, chopped
2 tsp. paprika
1 tsp. chili powder
1 tsp. cumin
dash cayenne pepper
$1/2$ tsp. salt

Set aside.

Combine:
2 cups kidney beans
1 cup salsa

Partially bake at 375° F. for 10 minutes:
deep dish pie shell

Layer half of the meat in bottom of pie shell.
Top with half of the beans.
Repeat layers.

Sprinkle over top:
1 cup shredded cheddar cheese

Bake 375° F. for 25 minutes.

Remove from oven and top with:
1 cup finely chopped lettuce
1 tomato, chopped

Serves 6

Spiritual Nugget: Never be afraid to trust an unknown future to a known God.

63

TURKEY A LA KING

Saute in 2 Tbsp. olive oil:

1 onion, chopped

1 Tbsp. red bell pepper, chopped

1/2 cup chopped fresh mushrooms

Add and bring to a boil:

1 quart turkey or chicken broth

2 cups cooked turkey, chopped

1 tsp. salt

1/8 tsp. pepper

Stir 1/3 cup whole grain flour into 1/2 cup water.
Stir into boiling broth and boil 1 minute.
Remove from heat.

Add:

2 hard cooked eggs, diced

Serve immediately over toasted whole grain bread slices or biscuits.

Serves 8

WILD RICE PATTIES

Beat:

3 eggs

1/2 cup whole grain flour

2 tsp. dry mustard

1 tsp. coriander

1 tsp. salt

1/8 tsp. pepper

1/2 cup minced onions

1 cup cooked, chilled wild or brown rice

2 cups cooked, chilled brown rice

2 Tbsp. olive oil

Put 2 Tbsp. olive oil in heated skillet.
Cook patties on both sides until browned.

Optional: Place patties on baking pan. Bake 375° F. for 20 minutes.
Turn and bake 8 additional minutes.

Variation:

Add 1 1/2 cups shredded zucchini before mixing. Delicious!   Serves 7

YUMASETTI

Brown:
1/2 lb. ground beef

Add:
1 medium onion, diced   1/2 cup mushrooms, chopped
1 stalk celery, diced

Cook for 5 minutes, then stir in:
4 Tbsp. whole grain flour

Slowly add, while stirring and cooking:
1 quart tomato juice

Cook and stir for 2 minutes after bubbly.

Add:
1 tsp. paprika   1 tsp. salt
1 tsp. chili powder

Combine with 1 lb. whole grain noodles, cooked according to directions.
Pour into casserole.
Bake covered 350° F. for 30 minutes.
If refrigerated, bake for 1 hour.   Serves 6

ZUCCHINI AND MUSH

In a large skillet, cook uncovered, until zucchini is tender:
1 medium zucchini, diced   1 tsp. salt
1 quart chunk tomatoes   dash pepper
1 onion, diced

Meanwhile, make cornmeal mush in skillet.

Bring to a boil:
4 cups water

Combine:
2 cups yellow cornmeal   1 tsp. salt
2 cups cold water

Stir into boiling water. Boil and stir until mush thickens.
Pour 1/4 of the mush into a greased 9 x 13" pan.
Cover with vegetables. Spread remaining mush over vegetables.
Bake 350° F. for 1 hour.   Serves 8 - 10

ITALIAN ZUCCHINI

In skillet, saute in 1 Tbsp. olive oil:
1 medium onion, diced

Add:
6 cups sliced zucchini (no need to peel)
1 cup chopped tomatoes
1/2 tsp. salt
1/4 tsp. Italian Seasoning
1/8 tsp. pepper

Cover and cook on low until tender, about 30 minutes, stirring several times.

ZUCCHINI PIZZA

Beat:
6 eggs

Add:
3 cups shredded zucchini
1 cup whole grain flour
1/2 tsp. basil
1/2 tsp. oregano
1/2 tsp. salt
dash pepper

Pour onto greased 14" pizza pan.
Bake 450° F. for 8 minutes or until set.
Spread pizza sauce over top.

Sprinkle desired amounts of the following over pizza sauce:
chopped bell pepper
chopped onion
chopped mushrooms
chopped tomatoes
shredded cheese

Lower oven temperature to 350° F.
Bake 350° F. for 10 minutes or until cheese is melted.

Meats

ITALIAN OVEN FRIED CHICKEN
(Also delicious on fish)

In skillet, saute in 2 Tbsp. olive oil:
1 Tbsp. minced onion

Tip:
Always
discard skin
and fat from
chicken
before
baking or
cooking.

Add:

1 Tbsp. dried parsley

2 tsp. Italian Seasoning

$^1/_2$ tsp. salt

$^1/_4$ tsp. pepper

$^1/_4$ tsp. dry mustard

2 cups whole grain bread crumbs

Stir well to coat crumbs. Continue stirring and cooking until browned, 5 - 10 minutes. Finely crumble the crumbs in blender.
Dip chicken, (3 - 3$^1/_2$ lbs.) or fish, (about 2 - 2$^1/_2$ lbs.) into a beaten egg, then coat with crumbs. Lay single layer on baking pan.
Bake uncovered. Chicken 350° F. for 1 hour.

Fish   450° F. for 15 - 20 minutes.   Serves 8

SWEET AND SOUR CHICKEN

Place in crock-pot:
1 whole chicken or cut up chicken pieces
1 onion sliced and separated into rings

Combine and pour over chicken:
1 cup ketchup
2 Tbsp. vinegar
1 red bell pepper, cut into short strips
$^1/_2$ tsp. salt
$^1/_4$ tsp. stevia
1 - 20 oz. can pineapple chunks with juice

Tip:
Poultry
spoils quickly.
Defrost in refrigerator,
or unwrapped
in cold water.
Cook promptly.
Refrigerate
leftovers
immediately.

Optional:
Put medium sized unpeeled potatoes on top of chicken.
Cook covered on low for 5 hours, then switch to high for 1 hour, or cook on low for 7 hours.

Note:
Use leftover chicken and broth mixture for Chicken Vegetable Soup (page 80) in place of part of the broth.

CHICKEN TURNOVERS

Delicious for those special occasions!

Saute in 1 Tbsp. olive oil:
1 Tbsp. chopped onion

Stir in:
2 Tbsp. whole grain flour
2 Tbsp. water
1 cup chopped cooked chicken
1½ Tbsp. mayonnaise
pinch garlic powder
¼ tsp. salt
dash pepper

Set aside.

Cut back on fat in hamburger patties: Place on greased baking sheet. Bake at 400°F. for 35 minutes. Drain.

PASTRY

In mixer bowl, combine until crumbly:
1½ cups whole grain flour
½ tsp. salt
½ tsp. paprika
¼ cup olive oil

While slowly mixing, gradually add:
4 - 5 Tbsp. cold water

On a floured surface, roll out dough, ¹/₁₆ inch thick.
Cut in 3 inch circles.
Drop a heaping tsp. of chicken mixture on half of each circle.
Moisten edges with water.
Fold dough over filling, and press edges with fork.
Prick tops with fork.
Place on baking sheet.
Bake 375° F. for 20 minutes or until browned.

Yields 18

SPINACH CHICKEN ROLLUPS

Thaw:
9 boneless chicken breasts

Saute in 1 Tbsp olive oil:

1 small onion, chopped   1 garlic clove, minced
$1/2$ cup fresh chopped mushrooms

Add:

2 cups cooked, chopped spinach $1/2$ tsp. salt
$1/2$ tsp. oregano $1/4$ tsp. pepper

Combine and place in middle of chicken, clear across, shortways.
Start at small end, and roll over spinach.
Bring other end over, and insert toothpick to hold together.

Combine:

$1/2$ cup fine bread crumbs $1/2$ tsp. paprika

Roll chicken rolls in beaten egg, then in crumbs.
Place on baking pan.
Bake uncovered 350° F. for 1 - $1/2$ hours depending on size of chicken breasts.

> **Spinach**
> is an excellent source of vitamin A and C, and a fair amount of B. It has a large amount of fiber, and is a mild laxative.

ALMOND BAKED FISH

In a shallow dish, mix:

$3/4$ cup whole grain flour $1/8$ tsp. pepper
$3/4$ tsp. salt

In another shallow dish, beat:

2 eggs   1 Tbsp. lemon juice

In third shallow dish, combine:

$1 1/4$ cups fine whole grain bread crumbs $2/3$ cup chopped almonds

Dip into mixtures in order given:

$1 1/2$ lbs. fish filets, drained

Place on greased baking pan.
Bake uncovered 450° F. for 20 minutes.   Serves 6

BAKED FISH CAKES

In bowl, combine:

1½ cups flaked, cooked fish, drained
1½ cups thick mashed potatoes
1 egg, beaten
2 Tbsp. snipped parsley
2 Tbsp. minced onion

1 tsp. lemon juice
¼ tsp. celery seed
½ tsp. salt
⅛ tsp. pepper

Form into patties and roll in crumb mixture.

CRUMBS

In bowl, combine:

2 cups fine whole grain bread crumbs
2 Tbsp. snipped parsley

1 tsp. paprika

Bake uncovered on greased baking sheet 450° F. for 8 minutes.
Turn and bake an additional 8 minutes or until golden brown.   Serves 4

For an inexpensive yet "good tasting" fish, try Frozen Alaskan Pollock filets.

PAN FRIED FISH

(When your husband comes home from fishing...)

Dip fresh filets in beaten egg. Roll in cornmeal.
Place skin side down in hot skillet greased with 2 Tbsp. olive oil.
Add salt and pepper to taste. Cover and cook, turning once.
Remove from skillet. Serve immediately.

FISH ROLLUPS

(A little messy to roll up, but delicious)

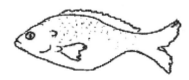

1 lb. fish filets

Mix:

⅓ cup chicken broth
1 Tbsp. olive oil
½ tsp. salt
pepper to taste

⅓ cup finely shredded or chopped carrots
1 Tbsp. green pepper, chopped
1 Tbsp. fresh parsley, snipped
2 cups bread crumbs

Divide onto filets. Spread over top.
Roll up from small end and secure with toothplck.
Put into baking dish. Bake 375° F. for 40 - 45 minutes.

FISH IN ORANGE SAUCE

Saute in 1 Tbsp. olive oil:
2 Tbsp. finely chopped onion

Stir together:
1 cup milk or water   1 tsp. grated orange peel
1 Tbsp. orange juice concentrate $1/2$ tsp. salt
3 Tbsp. whole grain flour $1/8$ tsp. pepper

Over medium heat while continuously stirring, slowly add flour mixture.
Continue stirring until thickened and bubbly.
Set aside.

Arrange in 9 x 13" greased baking pan:
2 lb. fish, thawed and drained

Pour sauce over fish.
Cover loosely, and bake 325° F. for 25 minutes or until fish flakes easily.

Serves 6

MACKEREL PIE

CRUST

2 cups cooked brown rice   1 egg white (save yolk for filling)
1 Tbsp. whole grain flour

Mix well and press into 9" pie pan.

Mix filling ingredients together:
2 eggs, slightly beaten   1 - 15 oz. can mackerel, drained
1 egg yolk, slightly beaten   1 Tbsp. snipped fresh parsley
$1/2$ cup milk or rice milk $1/8$ tsp. oregano
1 cup whole grain bread crumbs $1/8$ tsp. paprika
$1/4$ cup chopped onion $1/2$ tsp. salt
1 Tbsp. whole grain flour   dash pepper

Pour into rice crust.
Sprinkle lightly with additional paprika.
Bake uncovered 400° F. for 40 minutes.
Let set 10 minutes before cutting.

Spiritual Nugget:
A "little" evil is first a stranger, then a guest, then a master.

CURRY MEAT PIES

In skillet, brown:
1 lb. ground beef

Add:
1 onion, minced
1 Tbsp. curry powder, scant
1 Tbsp. chopped peppers

1 tsp. ginger
1 tsp. salt
$1/2$ cup pizza sauce

Stir together and set aside.

In mixer bowl, combine:
$3^1/2$ cups whole grain flour
2 tsp. baking powder
$1/4$ tsp. cream of tartar

$1/4$ tsp. salt
3 Tbsp. olive oil

Add:
1 cup cold water

Mix together until just combined.
On lightly floured counter, roll dough out $1/8$ inch thick.
Cut into 3 inch circles.
Place 1 Tbsp. meat on each circle. Fold in half.
Press edges together. Prick top with fork.
Optional: Brush lightly with egg white, and sprinkle sesame seeds over top.
Bake uncovered 350° F. for 25 minutes.   Yields 32 meat pies

> **Tip:**
> If you don't have round cookie cutters, use a drinking glass turned upside down.

ZESTY MACKEREL BURGERS

Mix together:
2 - 15 oz. cans mackerel, drained
4 eggs, beaten
1 cup rolled oats
1 Tbsp. minced onion
2 Tbsp. horseradish
$1/2$ tsp. red pepper
$1/4$ tsp. salt
dash pepper

Form into patties.
Cook covered, in a large greased skillet until browned on both sides.
                                        Serves 8 - 10

SPINACH MEATLOAF

In a bowl, combine:

2 lbs. ground turkey or beef
1 onion, chopped
2 eggs
$^1/_2$ cup sugar free ketchup
1 Tbsp. lemon juice
1 tsp. salt

$^1/_2$ tsp. pepper
1 tsp. basil
$^1/_2$ tsp. oregano
2 cups chopped cooked spinach
2 cups fine bread crumbs

Form into a loaf in a 9 x 13" pan.
Spread salsa over top.
Bake uncovered 350° F. for 1 hour.

Serves 12

SALMON PIE

Beat:
3 eggs

Add:
$^1/_2$ cup milk or rice milk
$^1/_4$ cup chopped onion
2 Tbsp. snipped parsley
1 Tbsp. olive oil
$^1/_2$ tsp. basil
$^1/_4$ tsp. salt
1 - 15 oz. can salmon or mackerel, drained

Don't remove the bones from canned mackerel and salmon. They add calcium to your diet. Mash the drained salmon in a bowl with a fork. The bones are not detectable.

Mix well. Pour into 9" pie pan.
Bake uncovered 425° F. for 25 minutes.
Cut into wedges to serve.

Serves 6

FORM YOUR OWN GRAVY

Cook together with steak or chunk beef:

2 cups water
4 Tbsp. minute tapioca
$^1/_2$ tsp. poultry seasoning

1 tsp. salt
$^1/_4$ tsp. pepper

Simmer covered for $1^1/_2$ hours or in crock pot on high for 5 hours, or low for 9 hours.

SAURKRAUT BALLS

Beat:
2 eggs

Add and mix well:

1 lb. ground sausage or beef
1 cup whole grain bread crumbs
1 Tbsp. diced onion
pinch garlic powder

1 Tbsp. snipped parsley
$1/8$ tsp. pepper
$2^1/2$ cups saurkraut, drained

Shape into $1^1/2$ inch balls.
Place in 9 x 13" pan.
Bake uncovered 400° F. for 35 minutes.
Serve with mashed potatoes.

Serves 8

Hint:
Ask your butcher to process bologna, sausage, and wieners, without sugar or MSG. Ask him to just add the spices such as salt, pepper, mustard, and garlic.

√ TURKEY VEGGIE BURGERS

In a bowl, combine:

2 lbs. ground turkey
2 cups shredded zucchini
1 carrot, grated
2 Tbsp. minced onion

3 Tbsp. sugar free ketchup
1 Tbsp. mustard
$1/2$ tsp. salt
$1/8$ tsp. pepper

Shape into patties and place on greased baking pan.
Bake uncovered 400° F. for 35 minutes.
Serve with bread, tomato slice, and lettuce.

Serves 8

√ BARBECUE SAUCE
(Delicious on grilled or oven baked chicken or hamburgers.)

In a small sauce pan, combine:
2 cups sugar free ketchup
$1/4$ cup white grape raspberry juice concentrate
2 tsp. lemon juice
2 tsp. vinegar
1 Tbsp. minced onion
1 tsp. finely minced garlic
$1/2$ tsp. dry mustard

Simmer 10 minutes.

Enough for about 6 quarters

CITRUS MARINADE

Combine and set aside:
1 Tbsp. white grape juice concentrate
1 lemon, juiced
1 orange, juiced

In saucepan, combine
2 tsp. olive oil
$1/4$ cup minced onion
1 tsp. minced garlic
1 tsp. fresh or $1/2$ tsp. dried thyme
$1/2$ tsp. salt
dash pepper
$1/2$ cup water

Bring to a boil over medium heat.
Turn to low and simmer 10 - 15 minutes. Stir fruit juice in.
Marinate chicken breasts or fish for at least 8 hours.
Don't rinse marinade off.
Coat with flour, salt, and pepper, or crushed fruit juice sweetened corn flakes.
Place single layer on baking pan.
Bake uncovered: Chicken 350° F. for 1 hour.
                 Fish   450° F. for 15 - 20 minutes.

Always marinate meats in the refrigerator. Discard after removing the meat. To reuse marinade, boil it first, to kill any bacteria from the meat.

VENISON MARINADE

Enough for up to 2 lbs. meat.

Marinating **meat** helps tenderize the meat and makes it easier to digest.

1 cup water
$1/3$ cup vinegar
2 Tbsp. lemon juice
1 Tbsp. oregano

1 tsp. garlic powder
$1/2$ tsp. salt
$1/2$ tsp. pepper

Marinate 2 hours or overnight.
Drain and discard marinade.

Soups

and

Sandwiches

CREAM OF BROCCOLI SOUP

In skillet, saute in 1 Tbsp. olive oil:

1 small onion, chopped   1 stalk celery, chopped

Add:

1 small head broccoli, chopped   2 cups chicken broth

Cover and simmer for 20 minutes. Remove $1/2$ cup of the broccoli pieces.
Puree soup in blender. Return to kettle.
Add broccoli pieces and bring soup to a boil.

Meanwhile, stir together:

1 cup water $1/4$ cup corn starch

Slowly stir cornstarch mixture into broccoli.

Stir in:

2 cups milk or rice milk   1 tsp. salt
$1/8$ tsp. thyme $1/8$ tsp. pepper

Continue stirring and heat until thickened and bubbly.   Serves 6

Don't add salt to beans while cooking. Add afterwards if adding salt.

BLACK BEAN SOUP

In large soup kettle, saute in 1 Tbsp. olive oil:

1 carrot, chopped
1 stalk celery, diced
1 onion, chopped

Add:

4 cups chicken broth
4 cups cooked black beans
1 cup shredded raw potatoes
$1/2$ tsp. oregano
$1/8$ tsp. garlic powder
$3/4$ tsp. salt
dash pepper

Simmer covered for 1 hour.   Serves 8

Quick Tip: Forget to soak your dry beans overnight? Cover beans with water. Cover and bring to a boil. Remove from heat and let set for 1 hour. Drain and cover with fresh water. Cover and cook for 1 hour, or until soft.

CABBAGE CAULIFLOWER SOUP

Saute in 2 Tbsp. olive oil 6 - 8 minutes:
1 large onion, chopped
1 clove garlic, minced
2 cups shredded cabbage

Add:
3 cups chicken or turkey broth
1 quart tomato juice
3 medium potatoes, cut in small cubes
1$^1/_2$ cups fresh cauliflower, cut in small florets

Bring to a boil.
Simmer covered for 20 minutes or until vegetables are tender.

Add:
$^3/_4$ tsp. salt
dash pepper

Stir in and serve.   Serves 8 - 10

CREAM OF CAULIFLOWER SOUP

In a medium soup kettle, bring to a boil:
$^3/_4$ cup water   2 large potatoes, diced
4 cups cauliflower florets

Simmer covered until soft, about 20 minutes.
Process in blender. Pour back into kettle.

Add:
4 cups chicken broth   1$^1/_4$ tsp. salt
$^1/_4$ tsp. nutmeg $^1/_8$ tsp. pepper

Simmer covered over low heat for 15 minutes.

Garnish with:
2 Tbsp. chopped, fresh chives   Serves 8 -10

Spiritual Nugget:
The man who only occasionally samples the Word of God will never acquire much of a taste for it.

CHICKEN VEGETABLE SOUP

One half hour before starting soup, soak 1/2 cup hulled barley in 1 cup water.

Deboning cooked **chicken?** Cut cooked chicken with scissors. **For turkey:** Lay a stack of meat on cutting board and cut with an electric knife.

In large soup kettle, combine and simmer covered for 1/2 hour:

1 quart tomato juice
4 cups broth
1 1/2 cups cooked navy beans
2 large carrots, sliced
1 large onion, chopped
1 stalk celery, chopped

2 Tbsp. chives, chopped, optional
1/4 tsp. marjoram
1/4 tsp. basil
barley, drained
2 cups cooked chicken or
    turkey, chopped

Add and simmer for 30 minutes longer:

1 cup peas
1 cup corn
1 cup green beans, opt.

1 1/2 tsp. salt
1/2 cup uncooked whole grain
    macaroni

Serves 12 -14

CREAMY CORN CHOWDER

In soup kettle, saute in 2 Tbsp. olive oil:

2 cups chopped cauliflower
1 stalk celery, chopped

1 onion, chopped

Add:

2 cups water
1 cup milk or rice milk

3 medium potatoes, small cubes

Simmer covered for 20 minutes.
Pour into blender. Process until smooth.
Pour back into kettle.

Add:

1 quart corn
1 1/4 tsp. salt

1/8 tsp. pepper

Heat through.

Serves 6 - 8

FISH CHOWDER

Saute in 2 Tbsp. olive oil:

1 medium onion, diced   2 stalks celery, chopped

Add:

1 lb. fish, cut in small pieces   2 large carrots, diced
1 quart tomato juice $1/4$ tsp. dry mustard
4 medium potatoes, cubed $1/2$ tsp. thyme

Simmer covered for 30 - 35 minutes or until potatoes are tender.

Season with:

1 tsp. salt
pepper to taste

Variation:

Substitute 3 cups water and 1 cup milk or rice milk for the quart of
tomato juice. Blend 2 cups of the chowder and return to kettle.
Bring to a boil and serve.   Serves 8

LENTIL PASTA SOUP

In soup kettle, saute in 1 Tbsp. olive oil:

1 stalk celery, diced   1 onion, chopped
1 carrot, diced   1 garlic clove, minced
2 Tbsp. diced bell pepper

Add:

3 cups broth   1 cup lentils
3 cups water $1/2$ tsp. salt

Simmer covered for 30 minutes.

Add:

4 oz. uncooked whole grain macaroni
1 cup frozen, chopped spinach, thawed

Simmer covered for 12 minutes or until pasta is tender.   Serves 6 - 8

Food for Thought:
You cannot do a kindness too soon, because you never know how soon it will be too late.

LENTIL RICE SOUP

In a large soup kettle, saute for 3 - 4 minutes in 2 Tbsp. olive oil:
1 medium onion, chopped
1 garlic clove, minced
1 medium pepper, chopped
2 stalks celery, diced

Add and saute for 3 - 4 minutes longer:
1/2 cup uncooked brown rice

Add:
1 cup dry lentils
2 cups broth
3 cups water
1 tsp. thyme
1 tsp. salt
dash pepper

Simmer covered for 45 minutes.   Serves 6 - 8

Spiritual Nugget: God answers Kneemail.

LENTIL SOUP

In soup kettle, saute in 1 Tbsp. olive oil:
1 cup chopped onions
1 large carrot, chopped
1 garlic clove, minced

Add:
1 quart tomato juice or chunks
1 quart chicken broth
2 cups uncooked lentils
1 tsp. salt
1/2 tsp. thyme
pepper to taste

Simmer covered for 1 1/2 hours.

Add and serve:
2 Tbsp. parsley, snipped   Serves 8

MINESTRONE

In large soup kettle saute in 2 Tbsp. olive oil until just tender:
2 medium potatoes, diced   1 medium carrot, chopped
1 small onion, diced

Add and saute until just tender:
2 cups zucchini, sliced

Add:
2 cups water   dash garlic powder
1 quart canned chunk tomatoes   1 tsp. salt
1 tsp. basil   dash pepper
1/2 tsp. oregano

Simmer covered for 15 minutes.

Add:
4 oz. whole grain spaghetti, broken in pieces

Simmer for an additional 12 - 15 minutes.   Serves 6 - 8

NOODLE SOUP

In soup kettle, saute in 1 Tbsp. olive oil for 3 minutes:
1 stalk celery, diced
1/4 cup chopped carrots
1 small onion, minced

Add:
1 quart chicken or turkey broth
3 cups water
1/2 tsp. salt

Bring to a boil.

Add:
8 oz. whole grain noodles

Simmer covered for 20 minutes.   Serves 8

To remove fat swimming on cooled broth: Skim a paper towel over. Or freeze to harden fat. When partially thawed, remove fat.

√ CHUNKY POTATO SOUP

In soup kettle, brown:
1 lb. ground beef

Add:
4 cups chunked potatoes
1 quart canned chunk tomatoes
$^3/_4$ cup water
2 tsp. salt
$^1/_2$ tsp. pepper

Bring to a boil and simmer for 1 hour.   Serves 6 - 8

CREAMY POTATO SOUP

In soup kettle, saute in 2 Tbsp. olive oil:
1 onion, chopped
1 garlic clove, minced

Add:
$^1/_3$ cup whole grain flour

While continuing to stir, add:
4 cups water

Reduce heat and add:
6 medium potatoes, diced
2 cups cubed bologna, sausage, or weiners

Cover and simmer over low heat for 30 minutes,
or until potatoes are tender.

Add:
1 cup milk or rice milk
1 tsp. salt
pepper to taste

Heat.
Garnish with parsley to serve.   Serves 10

Hint:
Ask your butcher to process bologna, sausage, and wieners without sugar or MSG. Ask him to just add the spices such as salt, pepper, mustard, and garlic.

HEARTY POTATO SOUP

In soup kettle, brown:
1/2 lb. ground beef, optional

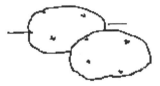

Add:
1 medium onion, chopped
1 cup thinly sliced carrots
1 Tbsp. chopped green pepper
2 cups potatoes, diced
2 cups tomato juice

Simmer covered until vegetables are tender, about 25 minutes.

Combine:
2 cups milk or rice milk
1/3 cup whole grain flour
1 1/2 tsp. salt
1/8 tsp. pepper

Add to soup, stirring constantly. Heat, but do not boil.   Serves 6

PARSLEY POTATO SOUP

In soup kettle, saute in 2 Tbsp. olive oil until just tender:
1 onion, chopped
1 stalk celery, chopped
1/2 cup chopped parsley

Add and simmer covered for 20 minutes:
4 cups chicken or turkey broth
6 medium potatoes, finely diced

Combine:
1 cup milk or rice milk
1 tsp. salt
3 Tbsp. whole grain flour
1/2 tsp. lemon juice
1/8 tsp. pepper

Slowly pour into simmering soup, stirring constantly.
Bring to a boil and continue stirring for 1 minute. Serve.   Serves 8

Food for Thought:
Good character, like good soup, is usually homemade.

SALMON CHOWDER

In soup kettle, heat:
1 Tbsp. olive oil

Add and cook, stirring occasionally for about 10 minutes:
2 cups finely diced carrots   ¹/₂ cup finely chopped onion
¹/₂ cup diced celery

Add:
4 cups chicken broth   3 cups cubed potatoes
1 cup water   (about ¹/₂ inch)

Cook covered for 15 minutes or until potatoes are tender.

Stir together:
³/₄ cup milk, rice milk, or water   2 Tbsp. corn starch

Add and cook, stirring until bubbly.

Add:
1 - 6 oz. can pink salmon   ³/₄ tsp. salt
¹/₄ tsp. dill

Heat through.   Serves 8

SAVORY SPLIT PEA SOUP

Before starting soup, soak ¹/₂ cup hulled barley in 1 cup water for ¹/₂ hour.

In soup kettle, saute in 1 Tbsp. olive oil:
1 onion, chopped   2 cups thinly sliced carrots
1 stalk celery, chopped

Add:
4 cups chicken or turkey broth   2 large bay leaves
1 quart cooked northern or navy beans ¹/₈ tsp. garlic powder
1¹/₄ cups dry split peas   soaked barley, drained

Bring to a boil.
Lower heat, and simmer covered for 1 hour.

Add:
3 cups chopped cabbage

Simmer for ¹/₂ hour longer. Remove bay leaves.

Add and serve:
1¹/₂ tsp. salt   ¹/₈ tsp. pepper

Serves 12

TURKEY BEAN & BARLEY SOUP

Before starting soup, soak 1/2 cup hulled barley in 1 cup water for 1/2 hour.

Bring to a boil and simmer covered for 1 hour:

4 cups turkey broth or water	2 cups cooked turkey or chicken, chopped
barley and soaking water	5 bay leaves
2 cups cooked navy beans	1/2 tsp. marjoram
1 large carrot, diced	1/4 tsp. thyme
1 stalk celery, chopped	1/4 tsp. dry mustard
1 medium onion, diced	1 1/4 tsp. salt
1 garlic clove, minced	1/8 tsp. pepper

Last 1/2 hour, add:
2 cups green beans

Before serving, add:
2 Tbsp. chopped parsley

Remove bay leaves and serve.   Serves 8

CREAM OF MUSHROOM SOUP

Use in place of "Campbell's Mushroom Soup."

Spread over meatballs to bake or add to casseroles.

> **TIP:**
> Commercially canned soups are high in sodium, contain bad fats, MSG, and food additives.

Saute in 1 Tbsp. olive oil:

2 Tbsp. finely chopped onions	12 ounces fresh mushrooms,
1 garlic clove minced	finely chopped

Add and bring to a boil:

1 tsp. thyme	1/4 tsp. pepper
1 tsp. parsley	2 cups chicken broth
1/2 tsp. salt	

Blend together:

1 cup milk or rice milk	1/2 cup whole grain flour

Stir milk into boiling broth. Cook and stir for 3 minutes.
Leftovers can be frozen for later use.

TURKEY CURRY SOUP

In large soup kettle, saute in 1 Tbsp. olive oil until tender:

1 onion, chopped
1 stalk celery, chopped

2 Tbsp. chopped red bell pepper
2 cups chopped carrots

Add:

2 cups cooked turkey, chopped
2 cups chopped cabbage
1 peeled apple, finely chopped

1 cup chopped zucchini
4 cups turkey broth or water

Simmer covered for 40 minutes.

In blender, process:

1 cup milk, rice milk, or water

1 - 16 oz. can garbanzo beans, drained

Add to soup at end of cooking time:

1 1/2 tsp. curry powder
1 1/2 tsp. salt

dash pepper
blended garbanzo beans

Heat and serve.

Serves 10

VEGETARIAN CHILI

Combine in soup kettle:

1 cup broth
1 cup chopped carrots
1 onion, chopped

Simmer covered for 10 minutes.

Add:

1 quart tomato juice
4 cups cooked black beans or pinto beans
4 cups cooked kidney beans
2 tsp. chili powder
1 tsp. salt

Bring to a boil. Simmer covered for 20 minutes.

Serves 10

OPEN-FACED FISH MELT

Cook 20 minutes or until fish flakes:
1 lb. fish

Flake fish and drain well.
Preheat oven to broil.

Add:

2 Tbsp. chopped red bell pepper   1 tsp. salt
2 stalks celery, chopped $1/8$ tsp. pepper
4 Tbsp. mayonnaise or salad dressing

Toast 6 - 8 slices of whole grain bread.

Place on top of toast:
1 tomato slice
fish mixture
1 slice of cheese

Place sandwiches on baking pan.
Broil on top rack for 2 - 3 minutes or until cheese melts.

Spiritual Nugget:
God loves each of us as if there was only one of us to love.

BAKED SALMON SANDWICHES

Combine:

2 - 6 oz. cans salmon, drained   2 Tbsp. pickle relish
$1/4$ cup mayonnaise   2 tsp. lemon juice
1 Tbsp. minced onion $1/4$ tsp. salt

Spread on toasted whole grain buns or bread.
If desired, put a slice of cheese on top.
Bake 450° F. for 5 - 10 minutes or until cheese is melted.

Yields 5 sandwiches

SAILBOATS

Make Hamburger Buns (page 26) ahead of time.

In a bowl, combine:

1 - 6 oz. can tuna, drained $1/4$ cup mayonnaise
1 small apple, chopped $1/4$ tsp. salt
2 Tbsp. chopped celery

Set aside. Place 6 hamburger bun halves on serving platter.
Place a lettuce leaf on each half. Top with tuna mixture.
Place 2 tortilla chips upright on sandwich for sails.   Yields 6 sandwiches

PIZZA SLOPPY JOES

In large skillet, brown:
2 lbs. ground beef

Drain fat and add:
1 medium onion, chopped

Cook until clear.

Stir in:

2 Tbsp. whole grain flour	1 tsp. salt
1 tsp. chili powder	2 cups pizza sauce
1 tsp. dry mustard	1 cup catsup
$1/4$ tsp. garlic powder	2 Tbsp. chopped green pepper
$1/4$ cup fresh chopped mushrooms	
or 1 - 4 oz. can, drained	

Bring to a boil.
Reduce heat and simmer uncovered for 20 minutes or until desired thickness.
Serve on whole grain buns or bread.   Yields 10 - 12 sandwiches

CREAMY TUNA SANDWICH

In medium skillet, combine:

2 cups water	2 Tbsp. diced onion
4 Tbsp. whole grain flour	

Cook on medium heat, stirring constantly until thickened.

Stir in:
1 cup frozen peas, thawed and drained
1 cup cooked, diced carrots
3 - 6 oz. cans tuna, drained

Heat.
Toast whole grain bread in oven or toaster.
Spread tuna on bread.
If desired, top with a thin slice of cheese.
Place under broiler until cheese is melted. It doesn't take long!

Yields about 9 sandwiches

Vegetables

BUTTERNUT SQUASH

Peel squash. Slice neck portion of squash ⅛ inch thick.

Heat large skillet and add:
2 Tbsp. olive oil

Dip slices in additional olive oil, and then into a combination of:
whole grain flour
salt
pepper

Fry covered, single layer, until browned and tender, turning one time.
Add 1 Tbsp. olive oil before frying next panful.

Note:
Use in place of pumpkin in recipes.
Cut bottom portion of squash in chunks, removing seeds.
Cook about 45 minutes or until soft.

BAKED CABBAGE DELUXE

In large skillet, over medium-high heat, combine:

2 Tbsp. olive oil   1½ cups whole grain bread crumbs

Stir constantly for 5 - 6 minutes.
Remove from skillet and set aside.

> **Potato Skins**
> are rich in
> vitamin B, C,
> and minerals.
> Leave them
> on whenever
> possible.

To skillet, add:

2 Tbsp. olive oil   1 Tbsp. minced onion
1 stalk celery, chopped   6 cups finely chopped or shredded
                                                                    cabbage

Saute for 5 - 6 minutes, stirring occasionally.
Remove from heat.

Add:

1 large peeled tomato, chopped   ⅛ tsp. pepper
½ tsp. salt   bread crumbs

Stir together and pour into casserole dish.
Bake 350° F. for 40 minutes or until cabbage is just tender.   Serves 8

BAKED RED BEETS

(Very tasty. No need to add salt or butter)

Wrap each red beet in foil, shiny side in.
Leave about $1/2$ inch of top and bottom on so it doesn't bleed.
Place in a baking pan.
Bake 400° F. for 1 - $1^1/_2$ hours depending on size of beets.
To test if soft, pierce with a paring knife. Peel in cold water.
Cut in chunks or slices. If desired, add salt or lemon juice.
Serve warm.

CALICO CABBAGE

Place in greased casserole:
1 small head cabbage, chopped
3 carrots, shredded
1 onion, chopped

Sprinkle over top:
2 tsp. lemon juice
1 tsp. salt
$1/_8$ tsp. pepper

Bake covered 375° F. for 30 minutes.   Serves 10

CARROTS AND SNOWPEAS

Place in medium sauce pan in order given:
water to cover bottom of pan
2 cups sliced carrots
2 cups snow peas, bite size

Simmer covered, 20 minutes or until just tender.

**Do not
overcook
vegetables.**
Serve tender-crisp.
To preserve vitamins,
cook vegetables
waterless or steam
if possible.

Add:
1 Tbsp. lemon juice
$1/_2$ tsp. salt

Stir well.

Sprinkle over top to serve:
$1/_4$ cup slivered almonds   Serves 6

93

CORN FRITTERS

In a bowl, combine:

1 1/2 cups sweet corn	1 tsp. cumin
2 Tbsp. chopped pepper	1/4 tsp. salt
1 onion, chopped	1/8 tsp. pepper
1 1/4 cups whole grain flour	1 cup milk or rice milk
2 tsp. baking powder	

Heat skillet, and grease with olive oil.
Pour in batter like for pancakes.
Brown on both sides.   Serves 8

SAUCY GREEN BEANS

In kettle, saute in 1 Tbsp. olive oil:

1 red bell pepper	1 garlic clove, minced
1 Tbsp. chopped onion	

Add:

1 Tbsp. water	1/2 tsp. salt
2 tsp. vinegar	1/8 tsp. pepper
1 tsp. mustard	

Stir together.

Add:
1 quart green beans

Heat and serve.   Serves 8

OVEN FRENCH FRIES

6 medium potatoes, cut french fry style

Mix together:

2 Tbsp. olive oil	1 tsp. salt, optional
2 tsp. Italian Seasoning	

Pat potatoes dry with paper towel.
Place potatoes in large sealable container.
Drizzle with oil mixture. Cover and shake well to coat.
Spread out single layer on cookie sheet.
Bake 450° F. for 30 - 40 minutes.   Serves 6

CRISPY JO JO'S

Cut into wedges:
8 medium potatoes

Combine in sealable bowl:

3 Tbsp. olive oil
1/2 tsp. salt

1/4 tsp. pepper
1/2 tsp. garlic powder

Put a handful of potato wedges in bowl, cover, and shake to coat.
Place wedges on greased baking sheet.
Repeat process until all potato wedges are coated.
Bake 425° F. for 20 minutes, then turn with spatula.
Bake another 20 minutes or until golden brown.

POTATO CAKES

Combine:

4 cups raw shredded potatoes
2 large eggs
1/4 cup whole grain flour

1 small onion, chopped
1/2 tsp. salt
1/8 tsp. pepper

Drop onto greased baking pan.
Bake 375° F. for 15 minutes.
Turn cakes and bake an additional 10 minutes.
Serve with Barbecue Sauce (page 75), salsa, or ketchup.

**If you don't
have a garden:**
Buy frozen vegetables
rather than highly
salted canned
vegetables.

POTATO BALLS

In a bowl, combine:

3 cups mashed potatoes
2 cups fine bread crumbs
2 eggs
2 Tbsp. olive oil

2 Tbsp. chopped onion
1 small stalk celery, diced
salt and pepper to taste

Form into 1 1/2 inch balls.
Place on greased cookie sheet.
Bake 375° F. for 25 minutes.

Serves 8

FANCY BAKED POTATOES

(Pictured on front cover)

Cut medium size baking potatoes in half lengthwise.
Slice potatoes crosswise $\frac{1}{2}$ inches apart,
not quite all the way through, fanning potatoes slightly.
Place in baking pan. Brush potatoes with olive oil.

Sprinkle with desired amounts of the following:

paprika	pepper
salt	minced fresh parsley

Bake uncovered 375° F. for 70 - 90 minutes depending on size.

STEAMED BROCCOLI

In a large kettle, bring about 1 inch of water to a boil.

In a metal colander, place:
broccoli, bite size pieces

Shred a sweet apple over top.
Place colander in kettle so broccoli is above water level.
Cover and boil for about 4 minutes or until tender-crisp.
Serve immediately.

Fat free gravies: Freeze chicken or turkey broth to bring fat to the top. Partially thaw. Skim fat off and discard. Thicken broth with flour, cornstarch or clear jel, stirred into a little cold water.

DAIRY FREE MASHED POTATOES

Olive oil added in place of butter is delicious.
Use about half the amount you would of butter.
Use rice milk in place of milk.

GOLDEN BAKED POTATOES

Roll potatoes with skins on in olive oil, and place in baking pan.
Cover loosely with foil.

For variety, add a little garlic powder to the olive oil.
Bake 400° F. for 1 hour or until tender.

GARLIC MASHED POTATOES

Cook until soft:
8 large potatoes, peeled and chunked
2 garlic cloves, diced

In mixer bowl, beat until smooth.

Add:
1¼ tsp. salt
1 Tbsp. olive oil

Whip and serve immediately.

Trying to use less salt? Salt vegetables or potatoes after cooking. It takes less.

SCALLOPED POTATOES

Boil 10 large potatoes until just soft, but not mushy. Cool.

Meanwhile, in large skillet, heat on medium heat:
2 Tbsp. olive oil

Stir in:
3 Tbsp. whole grain flour   ⅛ tsp. pepper
1 tsp. salt

Continue stirring until smooth and bubbly.
Remove from heat.

Stir in:
2½ cups milk or rice milk

Return to heat. Boil for 1 minute, stirring constantly.
Remove from heat.

Add:
2 Tbsp. minced onion   2 Tbsp. chopped bell pepper

Add potatoes, peeled and sliced.
Pour into greased 9 x 13" baking pan.
Top with crushed "fruit juice sweetened cornflakes".
Bake uncovered 350° F. for 1 hour.   Serves 8 - 10

BROILED VEGGIE PATTIES

In a large bowl, combine:

1 egg, beaten
1 cup shredded zucchini
1/2 cup shredded carrots
1 Tbsp. minced onion
1 tsp. minced garlic

1/4 tsp. salt
2 cups black beans, mashed
1/2 cup bread crumbs
1 tsp. Italian Seasoning

Shape into patties. Place on greased cookie sheet. Preheat oven on broil.
Broil on top rack 6 minutes per side or until lightly browned.
Delicious on a slice of bread with tomato slice and lettuce.   Serves 8

VEGETABLE-GRAIN BURGERS

Cook for 1 hour:

1 cup brown rice
3 cups water

3/4 tsp. salt

Saute in 1 Tbsp. olive oil:

1/4 cup chopped onion
1 garlic clove, minced

1 stalk celery, diced
2 Tbsp. diced bell pepper

Stir into cooked rice.

Add:

1/4 cup oat bran
1/2 cup fine whole grain bread crumbs

1 Tbsp. minced parsley
1/2 tsp. salt

Set aside until cool enough to handle. Form into patties.
Brown in olive oil on both sides. Serve on buns with lettuce and tomato slice.
Serves 6

GRILLED VEGGIE MEDLEY

Combine vegetables and place in the middle of a large piece of foil:

1 small zucchini, sliced
1 large carrot, sliced
1/2 cup small broccoli florets
1/2 cup small cauliflower florets

1 onion, sliced and separated into rings
1 red bell pepper, coarsely chopped
1/2 cup fresh mushrooms, sliced

DRESSING

Combine:

1/4 cup olive oil
1 tsp. lemon juice
1 Tbsp. minced fresh parsley
1/8 tsp. garlic powder

1/2 tsp. basil
1/4 tsp. oregano
1/2 tsp. salt
dash pepper

Drizzle over vegetables, fold foil over, and seal tightly.
Grill over medium heat for 30 minutes or until tender.   Serves 4 - 6

ZUCCHINI FRIES

3 - 4 medium size zucchini

Cut in half lengthwise. Then $1/4$ inch lengthwise slices.
Finally, cut into $1/4$ inch sticks resembling french fries.

Beat just until soft peaks form:
1 egg white

Add zucchini fries and toss to coat evenly.

Combine in a tightly sealable bowl:

$1/2$ cup cornmeal $3/4$ tsp. salt
$1/4$ cup whole grain flour $1/8$ tsp. pepper
$1/8$ tsp. paprika

Place 1 handful of zucchini in bowl. Cover and shake to coat.
Place zucchini on greased baking sheet.
Repeat process.
Bake uncovered 400° F. for 15 - 20 minutes.   Serves 6 - 8

ZUCCHINI POTATO DISH

Place in greased 9 x 13" pan:

4 medium potatoes, thinly sliced $1/2$ tsp. salt
2 medium zucchini, thinly sliced   dash pepper
1 onion, thinly sliced into rings   3 Tbsp. olive oil
1 bell pepper, chopped

Toss together. Cover.
Bake 350° F. for 1 hour and 45 minutes or until potatoes are tender.
Serves 8

ZUCCHINI CARROT SUNSET

In heavy skillet, saute for 3 minutes in 1 Tbsp. olive oil:
2 cups thinly sliced carrots

Add and saute for 3 minutes longer:
6 cups sliced zucchini

Add $1/4$ cup water.
Cover and cook for 4 minutes or until tender crisp.
Add salt and pepper to taste.   Serves 5

STUFFED CARROTS

Place 1 inch of water in kettle and add:
12 medium carrots

Cover and bring to a boil. Simmer for 15 minutes or until tender-crisp.
Drain. Scoop out center of carrots, leaving a quarter inch shell.
Place on greased baking pan. Set aside.

In blender, process, leaving small pieces of carrots:

removed carrot pulp	2 tsp. horseradish
1 Tbsp. chopped onion	$1/8$ tsp. nutmeg
$1/4$ cup mayonnaise	pinch salt and pepper

Spoon into carrot shells. Sprinkle lightly with paprika.
Bake uncovered 375° F. for 20 minutes.   Serves 6

STUFFED ZUCCHINI

In large skillet, saute in 2 Tbsp. olive oil for 3 - 4 minutes:

$1/2$ cup uncooked brown rice	2 Tbsp. uncooked wild rice

Add and saute 3 minutes longer:

6 medium mushrooms, chopped	1 garlic clove, minced
1 stalk celery, diced	1 small onion, chopped

Add:
$1^2/3$ cups water

Simmer covered for 45 minutes. Remove from heat.

Add:

1 cup bread crumbs	1 tsp. oregano
1 cup pizza sauce	1 tsp. salt
2 Tbsp. parsley, snipped	$1/8$ tsp. black pepper

Mix together.
Cut 6 baby zucchini or 1 large zucchini in half length wise.
Scoop out pulp and seeds and discard. Place in baking pan.
Fill zucchini with rice mixture. Bake covered 375° F. for 1 hour for baby
zucchini, and $1^1/2$ hours for large zucchini or until soft.
Slice in 2 inch sections to serve.   Serves 6

Food for Thought: Many things are opened by mistake, but none so frequently as the mouth.

Salads

APPLE SLAW

In a bowl, combine:
1 small head cabbage, shredded
5 sweet apples, finely diced (no need to peel)
2 Tbsp. finely chopped celery

DRESSING

In blender, process:
3 Tbsp. vinegar	1 tsp. salt
2 Tbsp. apple juice concentrate	1 tsp. stevia
2 Tbsp. olive oil	1/2 tsp. dry mustard

Stir dressing into salad.
Best if made the day before and refrigerated.

BROCCOLI PASTA SALAD

Cook according to directions:
10 oz. whole grain macaroni

Drain and rinse with cold water until cool. Drain well.

In a bowl, toss together:
2 cups finely chopped broccoli florets
2 large tomatoes, chopped
1 - 6 oz. can tuna, drained

In blender, combine:
2 Tbsp. white grape juice concentrate
3 Tbsp. vinegar
1 Tbsp. chopped onion
1/2 tsp. basil
1/2 tsp. oregano
1/2 tsp. salt

While processing on low speed, slowly pour in:
1/3 cup olive oil

Stir into broccoli. Add pasta and gently toss.
Refrigerate 2 - 3 hours to blend flavors.
Toss again before serving.

Tip:
Don't discard nutritious broccoli stems. Peel off the woody part and discard. Thinly slice stems and use in salads or soups.

BEAN SALAD

In serving bowl, combine:

2 cups canned green beans
1 cup canned pinto beans
1 cup canned navy beans

2 Tbsp. minced onion
1 Tbsp. finely chopped green pepper

DRESSING

In measuring cup, combine:

1/4 cup olive oil
4 Tbsp. vinegar
1/4 tsp. stevia

1 tsp. finely minced onion
1/4 tsp. dry mustard
salt to taste

Stir into beans.
Cover and refrigerate several hours or overnight to mingle flavors.
Stir before serving.   Serves 8

CARROT SALAD

Bring to a boil:

3 cups pineapple juice

Dissolve:

4 Tbsp. unflavored gelatin in 1 cup cold pineapple juice

Let set 3 minutes.
Stir gelatin into boiling juice, stirring until dissolved.
Remove from heat.

Add:

4 cups cold orange juice
1 - 20 oz. can crushed, canned pineapple, undrained
2 Tbsp. white grape juice concentrate
1 Tbsp. lemon juice
1/2 tsp. salt

Chill.

When almost set, add:

4 cups finely chopped or grated carrots

Chill.   Serves 18

COLESLAW

In a large bowl, combine:
5 cups shredded cabbage
2 carrots, shredded

1 red bell pepper, diced
1 small onion, minced

DRESSING

In blender, process:
1/4 cup mayonnaise, optional
1/4 cup white vinegar
2 Tbsp. white grape juice concentrate
2 Tbsp. mustard
1/4 tsp. celery seed

1/8 tsp. paprika
1/8 tsp. stevia
1/2 tsp. salt
dash pepper

Stir into cabbage and chill.
Best if chilled at least six hours.

CRANBERRY APPLE SALAD

In large bowl, combine:
1 large head Romaine lettuce, torn in small pieces
1 sweet apple, chopped
1 stalk celery, chopped
1/4 cup dried or fresh cranberries
1/4 cup slivered almonds or chopped walnuts

Toss. Add dressing just before serving.

DRESSING

2 Tbsp. apple cider vinegar
2 Tbsp. olive oil
1/4 tsp. rosemary
1/4 tsp. stevia
1/4 tsp. salt

Shake well. If refrigerated, oil becomes firm.
Allow to warm to room temperature.

CURRY CHICKEN SALAD

Combine:
1 head leaf lettuce
2 cups chopped, cooked chicken
1 cup frozen peas
1 cup cooked hulled barley
1 cup chopped, roasted peanuts
1 stalk celery, chopped
1 small onion, minced
1 carrot, shredded

Just before serving, stir in dressing.

DRESSING

Combine:
³/₄ cup mayonnaise
2 Tbsp. orange juice concentrate
2 tsp. dried mustard
1 tsp. curry powder

Spiritual Nugget:
In trouble and distress, Jesus speaks, saying, "Be of good cheer, it is I."

FISH CREOLE SALAD

In large skillet, saute 2 minutes in 2 Tbsp. olive oil:
1 green pepper, chopped
2 Tbsp. chopped onion
1 stalk celery, thinly sliced

Add:
4 cups tomatoes, peeled and chopped
1 lb. fish filets, cut in 1 inch pieces
2 Tbsp. vinegar
1 tsp. salt
¹/₄ tsp. marjoram
¹/₈ tsp. cayenne pepper
dash garlic powder

Cook for 15 minutes or until fish flakes easily.
Gently stir occasionally.
Serve over torn lettuce.

Serves 8

WINTER FRUIT SALAD

DRESSING

Combine in sauce pan:

1 egg, lightly beaten
2 Tbsp. cornstarch
2 Tbsp. orange juice concentrate

2 Tbsp. lemon juice
$1/2$ cup juice drained from pineapple

Bring to a boil over medium heat, stirring constantly.
Boil 2 minutes. Remove from heat.
Cool slightly. Stir into fruit.

Combine in bowl:

1 - 20 oz. can pineapple chunks
2 cups canned pears, chunked
2 bananas, sliced

2 oranges, sectioned and cut in half
2 cups seedless grapes
2 cups canned peaches, chunked

Chill for 2 - 3 hours.

Serves 8

Note:
Also delicious with fresh, chopped apples in place of peaches and pears.
Add $1/2$ cup pineapple juice to dressing.
Refrigerate before stirring into fruit.

ROSY FRUIT SALAD

DRESSING

In blender, process:
2 Tbsp. white vinegar
$1/4$ cup water

$1/2$ cup frozen red raspberries
$1/4$ cup white grape raspberry juice
concentrate

In bowl, combine:
5 sweet apples, chopped
2 bananas, sliced
1 orange, chopped

1 cup green seedless grapes
1 cup strawberries, halved, opt.

Stir dressing into fruit.

Serves 8

CITRUS FRUIT SALAD

Combine:
$1/4$ cup orange juice concentrate
1 Tbsp. lemon juice
juice drained from pineapple tidbits

Add:
1 - 20 oz. can pineapple tidbits, drained
3 red apples, diced, unpeeled
2 oranges, sectioned and cut in pieces
3 bananas, sliced

Stir well to be sure all the fruit is coated with juice.
Refrigerate at least 1 hour.
Stir before serving.   Serves 8 - 10

FRESH FRUIT SALAD

DRESSING

In blender, process until foamy:
2 eggs

Add and process:
2 tsp. whole grain flour
$1/2$ tsp. stevia
$1/2$ cup pineapple juice
$1/4$ cup lemon juice

Pour into heavy sauce pan.
Cook until just boiling, stirring constantly.
Cool.

Cut In bite size pieces:
3 apples
1 orange
1 banana
grapes

Stir cooled dressing into fruit.
Chill.   Serves 6 - 8

GARDEN SALAD

In serving bowl, combine:
1 head leaf lettuce, torn
1 carrot, finely shredded
1 cup flaked, cooked fish
1 tomato, chopped
2 radishes, thinly sliced

Toss and serve with French Dressing (page 117) or your favorite dressing.

LAYERED SALAD

Layer in order given in 8 x 8" square pan:
4 cups chopped leaf lettuce
1 small green pepper, finely chopped
2 cups elbow macaroni, cooked according to package directions
4 hard boiled eggs, diced
1 cup shredded red cabbage
1 small onion, minced
1 small carrot, shredded
1/2 lb. sausage, browned
1 cup frozen peas, thawed

Top with dressing.

Hint:
Ask your local butcher to process your venison or beef with salt and pepper, in place of the normal sausage seasonings!

DRESSING

Combine:
1 1/2 cups mayonnaise
1 Tbsp. white grape juice concentrate
1 Tbsp. mustard
1 tsp. horseradish
1/4 tsp. salt
dash pepper

Salad can be done the day before and refrigerated.   Serves 10

LETTUCE APPLE SALAD

(Pictured on front cover)

Toss together:
1 head leaf lettuce, torn
1 large apple, finely chopped
3/4 cup chopped pecans

Serve with Vinegar Celery Seed Dressing (page 117) or your favorite dressing.

LETTUCE WALDORF SALAD

DRESSING

In blender, process:
1/4 cup orange juice concentrate
1/2 tsp. lemon juice
1/2 cup mayonnaise
pinch salt

In serving bowl, combine:
4 sweet yellow apples, diced
1 stalk celery, diced
1 cup seedless red grape halves
1/2 cup chopped walnuts

Toss with dressing, and chill until ready to serve.

Just before serving, add:
3 cups torn leaf lettuce

Toss and serve.   Serves 8

WALDORF SALAD

Combine in medium sized bowl:
5 sweet apples, unpeeled, diced
1 cup finely chopped celery
1/3 cup raisins
1/4 cup chopped walnuts, optional

DRESSING

Combine:
1 Tbsp. orange juice concentrate
1 Tbsp. lemon juice
1/4 cup olive oil
1/4 tsp. cinnamon
1/4 tsp. dry mustard
1/2 tsp. salt

Stir into apples.
Can be made ahead of time and refrigerated.

MACARONI SALAD

Cook according to package directions:
12 oz. whole grain macaroni

Drain and rinse with cold water.

Tip:
When cooking macaroni for salad, rinse with cold water as soon as cooked, to stop cooking process.

Add:
6 hard cooked eggs, diced
2 medium carrots, finely chopped
1 sweet apple, finely diced

1 bell pepper, finely chopped
1 small onion, minced

Dressing:
1^1/$_2$ cups mayonnaise
^{1}/$_4$ cup milk or water
2 Tbsp. mustard
2 Tbsp. vinegar

^{1}/$_2$ tsp. stevia
1 tsp. salt
1 tsp. garlic salt
^{1}/$_2$ tsp. pepper

Refrigerate at least 2 hours before serving.
Leftovers are delicious and keep well in the refrigerator for up to 5 days.
Serves 12

MEDITERRANEAN SALAD

Your guests will enjoy this exotic salad!

Combine:
1 large head leaf lettuce
1 large tomato
1 - 2^1/$_4$ oz. can sliced black olives

1 medium red bell pepper, diced
^{1}/$_2$ cup shredded parmesan cheese

DRESSING

In blender, process:
1 Tbsp. chopped onion
2 Tbsp. vinegar
^{1}/$_2$ tsp. stevia

^{1}/$_2$ tsp. salt
^{1}/$_4$ tsp. dry mustard
^{1}/$_8$ tsp. oregano

While processing, slowly pour in:
^{1}/$_3$ cup olive oil

Toss with salad just before serving.

ORANGE TURKEY SALAD

In large bowl, combine:
1 head leaf lettuce, torn
1 medium scallion, minced
3 oranges, sliced and sectioned
1 cup cooked, chopped turkey or chicken
1/3 cup chopped pecans

Toss with dressing just before serving.

DRESSING

1/2 cup olive oil
1 Tbsp. orange juice concentrate
1 Tbsp. lemon juice
1 Tbsp. chopped onion

1/4 tsp. dry mustard
1/4 tsp. paprika
1/2 tsp. salt

Chill until ready to toss with salad.

ORANGE WHIP

Bring to a boil:
3 cups orange juice   1/4 tsp. salt

Dissolve 2 Tbsp. unflavored geletin in:
1/2 cup white grape juice concentrate

Stir into boiling juice.
Refrigerate until partially thickened, about 1 1/2 hours.
Pour into blender and process on high until fluffy.
Pour into serving bowl. Chill until firm.   Serves 6

√ SALMON SALAD

In serving bowl, combine:
1 head leaf lettuce, torn
1 - 6 oz. can boneless pink salmon
1 large tomato, chopped
1 hard cooked egg, diced
1 - 2 1/4 oz. can sliced black olives

Toss.
Delicious served with Russian Dressing (page 118) or your favorite dressing.

PICKLE SLAW

In a bowl, combine:
7 cups thinly sliced cucumbers
1 small onion, thinly sliced
1 Tbsp. chopped green pepper

DRESSING

Combine:
$1/4$ cup vinegar
2 Tbsp. white grape juice concentrate
$1/2$ tsp. celery seed
$1/2$ tsp. stevia

Stir dressing into cucumbers.
Cover and refrigerate overnight.   Serves 8

POTATO SALAD

Tip:
Always allow cooked potatoes to cool before shredding to avoid mushy potatoes.

Combine in large bowl:
2 lb. cooked, peeled, shredded potatoes
1 stalk celery, finely diced
2 Tbsp. chives or 1 Tbsp. minced onion
2 Tbsp. chopped red bell pepper

DRESSING

Combine:
$1\,1/2$ cups Dukes Mayonnaise or $3/4$ tsp. salt
     Mayonnaise (page 116)   dash pepper
1 Tbsp. mustard $1/4$ tsp celery seed
1 Tbsp. white vinegar

If too thick, add a little water.
Chill.
If desired, garnish with fresh parsley to serve.   Serves 8 - 10

TACO SALAD

Brown in covered skillet:
1 lb. ground beef

Add:

1 medium onion, chopped
2 cups kidney or pinto beans
1 tsp. paprika
1 tsp. cumin
3/4 tsp. chili powder

3/4 tsp. salt
1/8 tsp. pepper
dash garlic powder
1/2 cup tomato juice

Stir well.
Remove from heat.

In separate serving bowls, prepare:
1 large head leaf lettuce, torn
2 large tomatoes, chopped
1 1/2 cups shredded cheese
1 - 10 oz. bag corn chips or tortilla chips, broken.

On your individual plates, place lettuce.
Add meat-bean mixture.
Top with tomatos, cheese, and chips.
French Dressing (page 117) or your favorite salad dressing may be drizzled over top.

TURKEY GUACAMOLE SALAD

Place in large bowl:
1 medium head leaf lettuce, torn
2 cups chopped, cooked turkey
1 large tomato, chopped
1 ripe avocado, peeled and cut into 1/4 inch cubes

Toss salad.
Serve with Lime and Oil Dressing (page 117) or your favorite dressing.

Food for Thought:
Of all the troubles, great and small, the greatest are those that don't happen at all.

VEGETABLE PIZZA

Your guests will enjoy this.

CRUST

Place in measuring cup:

¹/₂ cup hot water   ¹/₄ cup white grape juice concentrate

When lukewarm, add:

1 Tbsp. yeast

Soak 5 minutes.

Beat:

1 egg

Add:

1 tsp. salt   yeast mixture

While mixing on low speed, slowly add:

1¹/₂ cups whole grain flour

Let rise ¹/₂ hour. Spread on greased jelly roll pan.
Bake 325° F. for 20 minutes. Cool.

FILLING

Beat together:

8 oz. cream cheese, softened   ¹/₂ cup sour cream or yogurt
1 tsp. chicken seasoning

While beating slowly, add:

1 cup Duke's Mayonnaise or Blender Mayonnaise (page 116)

Spread over cooled crust.

Sprinkle over top:

1 cup finely chopped broccoli   2¹/₂ cups finely chopped cauliflower
1 stalk celery, finely chopped   2 Tbsp. chopped bell pepper
3 fresh mushrooms, chopped

Top with 2 cups shredded cheddar cheese.
Finally, top with 1 small chopped tomato.
Chill.

TURKEY SALAD

Toss together:

1 head leaf lettuce, torn
1/2 cup shredded carrots

2 cups cooked turkey or chicken, chopped

Serve with Creamy Pineapple Dressing (page 116) or your favorite dressing. Garnish with slivered almonds.

VEGETARIAN TACO SALAD

Saute in 2 Tbsp. olive oil for about 5 minutes:

1 cup carrots, chopped
1 stalk celery, chopped
1 green bell pepper, chopped

1 small onion, chopped
1 garlic clove, minced
2 tomatoes, peeled and chopped

Add:

2 cups cooked kidney or pinto beans

Serve over torn lettuce.
Top with crumbled corn chips or tortilla chips.
Shredded cheese may be added.
French Dressing (page 117) or your favorite salad dressing may be poured over top.

Food for Thought: Strangers are just friends waiting to happen. Friends are the bacon bits in the salad bowl of life.

CROUTONS

Cut 6 slices of whole grain bread into small cubes.

In a measuring cup, combine:

1/4 cup olive oil

3/4 tsp. Italian Seasoning

Drizzle over bread cubes. Toss to evenly coat.
Spread out on cookie sheet.
Be sure to scrape oil and seasoning out of bowl, onto cubes.
Bake 275° F. for 1 hour or until crisp, turning twice.

BANANA POPPY SEED DRESSING

Delicious!

In blender, combine:

1 ripe banana
1 cup mayonnaise
2 tsp. poppy seeds

2 Tbsp. lemon juice
1/2 tsp. dry mustard
1/2 tsp. salt

Process until smooth. Chill.

BLENDER MAYONNAISE

In blender, process:

1 egg
2 Tbsp. vinegar
1 Tbsp. lemon juice
$1/2$ tsp. paprika

1 tsp. mustard
$1/2$ tsp. salt
$1/8$ tsp. stevia

Pour in very slowly while blending:
1 cup olive oil
(If you pour too fast, it won't thicken.)

Tip:
If you have not yet aquired a taste for olive oil, use part olive and part of another variety. Use unrefined cold pressed oil.

MAYONNAISE

In a heavy sauce pan or double boiler, combine:

3 Tbsp. whole grain flour
$1/4$ tsp. paprika

$1/4$ tsp. stevia
$1/2$ tsp. salt

In blender, process:

1 egg
1 tsp. mustard
2 Tbsp. olive oil

2 Tbsp. lemon juice
2 Tbsp. vinegar
$3/4$ cup water

Slowly stir into dry ingredients.
Stir and cook over medium heat just until mixture begins to boil.
Cool.   Yields 1 rounded cup

CREAMY PINEAPPLE DRESSING

In blender, process:
1 cup crushed pineapple with juice
1 Tbsp. white grape juice concentrate
$1/4$ cup Duke's Mayonnaise or Blender Mayonnaise
$1/2$ tsp. curry powder
$1/4$ tsp. salt

While blending, slowly pour in:
$1/4$ cup olive oil

FRENCH DRESSING
Place in blender:

1/3 cup catsup
1 Tbsp. mayonnaise
1 Tbsp. lemon juice

1 Tbsp. minced onion
1 tsp. stevia
1 tsp. salt

Process until smooth.

While processing, slowly pour in:
1/2 cup olive oil

VINEGAR CELERY SEED DRESSING
In blender, process:

1 tsp. chopped onion
1/4 cup vinegar
1 tsp. celery seed
1 tsp. dry mustard

1 tsp. paprika
1/2 tsp. stevia
1/2 tsp. salt

While blending, slowly add:
1 cup olive oil

LIME AND OIL DRESSING
Place in blender:

1/3 cup fresh lime juice
1/2 tsp. salt
1/8 tsp. pepper

While whizzing on low speed, slowly add:
1 cup olive oil

POPPY SEED DRESSING
In blender, process until smooth:

1/2 cup Duke's Mayonnaise or Mayonnaise (page 116)
1 Tbsp. vinegar
1/2 tsp. stevia
2 Tbsp. poppy seeds
pinch salt

RUSSIAN DRESSING

Process in blender, until smooth:
1 cup mayonnaise
2 Tbsp. salsa
1 Tbsp. finely chopped onion
1 Tbsp. parsley

Tip:
Cleaning the
blender or Vita-Mix:
Add a few drops of dish
soap. Fill almost halfway
with hot water. Run for a
short time. Rinse
and dry.

SWEET AND SOUR DRESSING

In blender, process:
1 Tbsp. chopped onion
1 small garlic clove
1 Tbsp. mustard
$1/4$ cup vinegar

1 tsp. celery seed
$1/4$ tsp. stevia
$1/4$ tsp. salt

While slowly processing, add:
$1/2$ cup olive oil

VINEGAR AND OIL DRESSING

In blender, combine:
3 Tbsp. white vinegar
1 tsp. salt
1 tsp. dry mustard

1 tsp. paprika
$1/4$ tsp. stevia
$1/8$ tsp. garlic powder

While blending on low speed, slowly pour in:
$3/4$ cup olive oil

CURRY VEGETABLE DIP

In blender, process until smooth:
1 cup mayonnaise
1 Tbsp. chopped onion
1 tsp. horseradish

2 tsp. lemon juice
$1/4$ tsp. garlic powder
$1/2$ tsp. curry powder

Refrigerate several hours before serving.

Cakes and Cupcakes

APPLE CAKE

Beat:

2 eggs

1/2 cup olive oil

1 cup apple sauce

1 tsp. vanilla

Add:

3 cups whole grain flour

1 tsp. baking powder

1 tsp. stevia

1/2 tsp. cinnamon

1/2 tsp. baking soda

1/4 tsp. cream of tartar

1/2 tsp. salt

Mix until just combined.

Fold in:

1 cup chopped pecans

3 cups chopped, peeled sweet apples

Place in a greased 8 x 12" pan.
Bake 350° F. for 45 minutes.

APPLE LAYER CAKE

Beat:

2 eggs

1 cup apple sauce

2 tsp. vanilla

Add:

2 1/2 cups whole grain flour

1 Tbsp. baking powder

1 tsp. salt

1 tsp. stevia

1/2 tsp. cinnamon

1/4 tsp. nutmeg

Mix until just moistened. Spread into two greased 8" round pans.
Bake 350° F. for 25 minutes. Remove from pans and cool.
Place one cake on plate.
Spread two cups apple pie filling over.
Cover with second cake.
Spread 1 cup pie filling over top.
Sprinkle with 1/3 cup chopped walnuts.

Food for Thought: The worst lies are those that most resemble truth.

120

APPLE SAUCE CAKE

In mixer bowl, beat:

1 egg
3 Tbsp. olive oil

1 cup apple sauce
1 tsp. vanilla

Add:

1 cup oat bran
1 cup whole grain flour
1 tsp. baking powder
³/₄ tsp. baking soda
2 tsp. cinnamon

1 tsp. stevia
¹/₂ tsp. allspice
¹/₂ tsp. ginger
¹/₄ tsp. cloves
¹/₄ tsp. salt

Mix together until just combined.

Fold in:

¹/₃ cup raisins

Pour into greased 8" pan.
Bake 375° F. for 25 minutes.

Spiritual Nugget:
To hear God's voice, turn down the world's volume.

APPLE STREUSEL COFFEE CAKE

CRUMBS

Combine and set aside:

¹/₂ cup whole grain flour
2 Tbsp. olive oil

¹/₄ tsp. stevia

Beat:

1 egg

¹/₂ cup olive oil

Add:

2 cups whole grain flour
¹/₂ tsp. baking powder
¹/₂ tsp. baking soda

1 tsp. stevia
³/₄ cup apple juice or water

Mix until just combined.
Spread two-thirds of the batter into a greased 8 x 12" pan.

Combine:

2 cups apple pie filling
¹/₂ tsp. cinnamon

¹/₂ cup raisins
1 tsp. lemon juice

Spoon over batter. Drop spoonfuls of remaining batter over filling.
Sprinkle crumb mixture over batter. Bake 350° F. for 1 hour.

ROMAN APPLE CAKE

TOPPING

Combine and set aside:

2 Tbsp. olive oil	1/4 tsp. stevia
4 tsp. whole grain flour	1 cup chopped nuts
1 Tbsp. cinnamon	

Beat:

2 eggs	1/2 cup apple sauce
1/2 cup olive oil	2 tsp. vanilla

Add:

3 cups whole grain flour	1 tsp. stevia
1 tsp. baking powder	1/2 tsp. salt
1/2 tsp. baking soda	1 cup apple juice

Mix until just combined.

Fold in:

6 medium sweet apples, peeled and chopped

Pour into greased 8 x 12" pan.
Sprinkle topping over cake.
Bake 350° F. for 55 minutes.

BANANA PRUNE CAKE

In blender, process:

2 eggs	1/2 cup prunes

In mixing bowl, combine:

prune mixture	1/4 cup water
1 cup mashed bananas	1 tsp. vanilla
1/2 cup olive oil	

Add:

2 cups whole grain flour	1/2 tsp. stevia
1 tsp. baking powder	1/2 tsp. salt
1/2 tsp. baking soda	3/4 cup chopped walnuts

Pour into greased 8 x 12" pan.
Bake 350°F. for 45 minutes.

APPLE WALNUT CAKE

Delicious!

TOPPING

Combine:

$^1/_2$ cup olive oil

1 cup whole grain flour

$^1/_2$ cup chopped walnuts

$^1/_2$ tsp. cinnamon

$^1/_4$ tsp. stevia

Set aside.

Beat:

1 cup olive oil

3 eggs

1 tsp. vanilla

Add:

2 cups whole grain flour

1 tsp. baking powder

1 tsp. baking soda

2 tsp. cinnamon

$1^1/_4$ tsp. stevia

$^1/_2$ tsp. salt

Mix until just combined.

Fold in:

1 cup chopped walnuts

4 cups chopped sweet apples

Place in greased 8 x 12" pan.
Spread topping over batter.
Bake 350° F. for 1 hour.

BLACK WALNUT SPICE CAKE

In mixer bowl, beat:

3 eggs

$^1/_2$ cup olive oil

Add:

3 cups whole grain flour

$1^1/_2$ tsp. baking soda

1 tsp. allspice

1 tsp. stevia

$^1/_2$ tsp. nutmeg

1 tsp. salt

$1^1/_4$ cups apple juice or water

1 cup chopped black walnuts

Mix until just combined.
Pour into greased 8 x 12" pan.
Bake 350° F. for 50 minutes.

Tip:
When baking, make a double batch and freeze some for emergencies or those busy days.

BLUEBERRY CAKE
CRUMBS

In small bowl, combine:

1 cup whole grain flour
1/2 tsp. cinnamon
1/4 tsp. stevia

1/3 cup chopped pecans
1/4 cup olive oil

Set aside.

In mixer bowl, beat:

2 eggs
1/4 cup olive oil

1/4 cup apple sauce
2 tsp. vanilla

Add:

2 cups whole grain flour
2 tsp. baking powder
1/2 tsp. salt

1/2 tsp. stevia
3/4 cup apple juice or water

Mix until just combined.
Spoon two-thirds of the batter into a greased 9" pie pan.
Sprinkle with two-thirds of the crumb mixture.
Top with 1 1/2 cups blueberries and remaining batter and crumbs.
Bake 350° F. for 1 hour and 10 minutes.
Cool slightly before removing from pan.

CARROT CAKE

Food for Thought:
Your personality will show twice the punch if you show interest in others instead of trying to get them interested in you.

Beat:

4 eggs
3/4 cup olive oil

1 tsp. vanilla

Add:

2 cups whole grain flour
2 tsp. baking soda
2 tsp. cinnamon

1 tsp. stevia
1 tsp. salt

Mix until just combined.

Fold in:

2 cups finely chopped or grated carrots
1 cup coconut

1 cup chopped nuts

Pour into greased 8 x 12" pan.
Bake 350° F. for 50 minutes.

BLACK FOREST CAKE

Moist & Delicious!

FILLING

In a saucepan, bring to a boil:
3$\frac{1}{2}$ cups sour cherries, with juice

Dissolve in $\frac{1}{2}$ cup apple juice:

4 Tbsp. cornstarch   1 tsp. cinnamon
1 tsp. stevia

Pour into boiling cherries while stirring constantly and cook for 1 minute.
Cool.

In mixing bowl, beat:

3 eggs $\frac{1}{2}$ cup olive oil

Add:

2$\frac{1}{4}$ cups whole grain flour $\frac{1}{2}$ tsp. stevia
$\frac{1}{3}$ cup carob powder   1 tsp. salt
1 tsp. baking soda   1$\frac{1}{4}$ cups apple juice

Fold sour cherry filling in.
Pour into greased 9 x 13" pan.

Sprinkle over batter:
1 cup chopped walnuts

Bake 375° F. for 50 minutes.

> Whole grains contain the entire grain kernel. (bran, germ, and endosperm) Refined grains have the bran and germ removed.

LEMON CUPCAKES

In mixer bowl, beat:

2 eggs   1 Tbsp. lemon juice
1 cup apple sauce $\frac{1}{4}$ cup olive oil

Add:

1$\frac{1}{4}$ cups whole grain flour $\frac{1}{2}$ tsp. baking soda
$\frac{3}{4}$ cup oat bran   1 tsp. stevia
1$\frac{1}{2}$ tsp. baking powder   1 tsp. grated lemon peel

Fill muffin tin lined with cupcake papers.
Bake 375° F. for 20 minutes.
Cool. Can be iced with Lemon Meringue Pie Filling. (page 164)

Yields 12 cupcakes

CRANBERRY COFFEE CAKE

FILLING

Boil:

2 cups cranberries

¹/₄ cup white grape juice

Mix:

¹/₂ cup white grape juice

3 Tbsp. cornstarch

Stir into boiling cranberries. Continue stirring until thick.
Set aside.

TOPPING

Mix together:

¹/₂ cup whole grain flour

¹/₂ tsp. stevia

¹/₄ cup slivered almonds

¹/₄ tsp. vanilla

2 Tbsp. olive oil

Set aside.

Sprinkle in round 8" pan:

¹/₄ cup slivered almonds

In mixing bowl, beat:

2 eggs

¹/₄ cup olive oil

¹/₄ cup apple sauce

1 tsp. vanilla

Add:

2 cups whole grain flour

1¹/₄ tsp. baking powder

¹/₂ tsp. baking soda

1 tsp. stevia

¹/₄ tsp. salt

Mix until almost combined.

Add:

1 cup milk or apple juice

Spread half of the batter in pan, put filling on, and spread the rest of
the batter on. Sprinkle topping on.
Bake 350° F. for 45 minutes.

GINGERBREAD

In blender, process:

1 cup apple juice or water
3 eggs
¼ cup orange juice concentrate

1 cup dates
1 tsp. vanilla
1 tsp. maple flavoring

Pour into mixer bowl.

Add:

2¾ cups whole grain flour
1 tsp. baking soda

2 tsp. ginger
1 tsp. cinnamon

Mix until just combined. Pour into greased 8 x 12" pan.
Bake 350° F. for 45 minutes.
(We like it best cooled to room temperature or refrigerated)

Tip:
For cakes that you remove from the pan after baking, instead of greasing the pan, line bottom with waxed paper, cut to fit.

RAISIN SAUCE

In blender, process:

1 cup water
½ cup dates
3 Tbsp. whole grain flour

½ tsp. stevia
pinch salt

Pour into saucepan.

Add:

1 cup raisins

1½ cups white grape or apple juice

Bring to a boil, stirring constantly. Cook 1 minute.

Add:

1 tsp. cinnamon

Serve hot over ginger bread.

MOLASSES GINGERBREAD

In mixing bowl, beat:

3 eggs
$\frac{1}{2}$ cup olive oil

$\frac{1}{3}$ cup blackstrap molasses
1 tsp. baking soda

Add:

$2\frac{3}{4}$ cups whole grain flour
1 tsp. cinnamon
1 tsp. ginger

$\frac{1}{2}$ tsp. stevia
1 tsp. vanilla
1 cup apple juice or water

Mix until just combined.
Pour into greased 8 x 12" pan.
Bake 350° F. for 30 minutes.

Tip:
Always preheat oven for accurate baking times.

FUDGY CAROB CAKE

Cherry topping adds a delicious touch to this cake.

In blender, process until smooth:

2 eggs
$\frac{1}{4}$ cup prunes

$\frac{1}{3}$ cup apple juice or water

Pour into mixer bowl.

Add:

1 cup whole grain flour
$\frac{1}{4}$ cup carob powder
1 tsp. baking powder

1 tsp. baking soda
$\frac{1}{2}$ tsp. stevia
$\frac{1}{2}$ cup chopped walnuts

Mix until just combined. Pour into greased 8 x 8" pan.
Bake 350° F. for 25 minutes.

CHERRY TOPPING

Bring to a boil:

2 cups sour cherries
$\frac{1}{2}$ cup apple juice

$\frac{1}{2}$ tsp. stevia

Stir in a mixture of:

4 Tbsp. white grape juice concentrate
2 Tbsp. clear jel

pinch salt

Bring to a boil while stirring continuously.
Boil for 2 minutes. Cool. Spread over top of cake.

CHERRY FILLED CUPCAKES

Mix filling and set aside to cool or use canned cherry pie filling.

FILLING

Bring to a boil:

1¹/₂ cups sour cherries
¹/₄ cup apple juice concentrate

¹/₂ tsp. stevia

Stir in a mixture of:

3 Tbsp. white grape juice concentrate
1¹/₂ Tbsp. clear jel

¹/₄ tsp. lemon juice
pinch salt

Bring to a boil while stirring continuously. Boil for 2 minutes.

In mixer bowl, beat:

3 eggs
¹/₂ cup apple sauce

¹/₂ cup olive oil
1¹/₂ tsp. vanilla

Add:

2¹/₄ cups whole grain flour
1¹/₂ tsp. baking powder

¹/₂ tsp. baking soda
1 tsp. stevia

Mix until just combined.
Fill muffin tin, lined with cupcake papers to ¹/₃ full.
Top each cupcake with a slightly rounded Tbsp. of cherry filling.
Spoon remaining batter over filling.
Bake 325° F. for 30 minutes.

Yields 1 dozen

ORANGE CAKE

Beat:

3 eggs
¹/₂ cup olive oil

2¹/₂ tsp. vanilla

Add:

4¹/₂ cups whole grain flour
1 cup oat bran
2 tsp. baking powder
2 tsp. baking soda

2 tsp. stevia
¹/₂ tsp. salt
2 Tbsp. grated orange peel
2 cups orange juice

Mix until just combined.
Spread in greased 9 x 13" pan. Sprinkle chopped pecans over top.
Bake 350° F. for 45 minutes.
Serve with milk or rice milk.

ORANGE ALMOND STREUSEL CAKE

STREUSEL

Combine:

3 Tbsp. olive oil
1 cup slivered almonds
1/4 cup whole grain flour

1 tsp. grated orange peel
1/4 tsp. stevia

Set aside.

In mixer bowl, beat:

3 eggs
1/2 cup olive oil

1 tsp. vanilla

Add:

2 cups whole grain flour
1 tsp. grated orange peel
1 1/2 tsp. stevia

1 tsp. baking powder
3/4 tsp. baking soda
2/3 cup orange juice

Spoon half of the batter into greased 10" tube pan.
Sprinkle with half the streusel. Top with the remaining batter and streusel.
Bake 350° F. for 35 minutes.
Cool. Remove from pan.

Tip:
Grated orange and lemon peel can be found at your local food co-op, bulk food store, or health food store.

PEAR CAKE

In blender, process:

1 cup dates
1 1/2 cups olive oil

3 eggs
2 tsp. vanilla

Pour into mixer bowl.

Add:

3 cups whole grain flour
1 tsp. baking soda
1 tsp. cinnamon
1/2 tsp. stevia

1 tsp. salt
1 Tbsp. coconut
3 cups pears, drained, chopped
1 cup chopped pecans

Mix until just combined.
Place in greased 8 x 12" pan.
Bake 350° F. for 1 hour.

PINEAPPLE PECAN CAKE

Beat:

3 eggs

1/2 tsp. vanilla

Add:

2 cups whole grain flour
1 tsp. baking soda

1 tsp. stevia
1 - 20 oz. can crushed pineapple

Mix until just combined.

Fold in:
3/4 cup chopped pecans

Pour into greased 9 x 13" pan.

Sprinkle over top:
1/4 cup chopped pecans

Bake 350° F. for 45 minutes.

PUMPKIN PECAN CAKE

In mixer bowl, beat:

2 cups pumpkin
3 eggs

1/2 cup olive oil
2 tsp. vanilla

Add:

2 cups whole grain flour
1 1/2 tsp. baking powder
1 tsp. baking soda
1 tsp. stevia

4 tsp. cinnamon
2 tsp. nutmeg
1/2 tsp. cloves
1 tsp. salt

Mix until just combined.

Fold in:
3/4 cup chopped pecans

Pour into greased 9 x 13" pan.
Sprinkle additional chopped pecans over top if desired.
Bake 350° F. for 45 minutes.

Food for Thought: Lost time is never found.

CAROB PEANUT BUTTER FROSTING

In saucepan, combine:

$\frac{1}{2}$ cup unsweetened peanut butter	1 Tbsp. olive oil
$\frac{1}{4}$ cup carob powder	1 tsp. vanilla
$\frac{1}{2}$ cup apple juice concentrate	

Cook over medium-low heat.

When it begins to bubble, add:
1 Tbsp. cornstarch dissolved in $\frac{3}{4}$ cup water

Cook, stirring constantly for 3 - 5 minutes.
Spread on brownies, cookies, or cupcakes.

Tip:
Sugar free frostings and icings aren't sweet like you may be accustomed to, but are nutritious and not nearly as fattening.

SEA FOAM FROSTING

Allow cake or cookies to cool before preparing frosting. Use immediately. Frosting on leftovers will shrink, but they are still good.

Combine in mixer bowl:

2 large egg whites, room temperature	$\frac{1}{8}$ tsp. cream of tartar
3 Tbsp. white grape juice concentrate	pinch of salt
1 tsp. vanilla	2 drops food coloring, opt.

Beat on medium-hi speed until frothy. Beat until firm, but not dry.
Spread on cooled cookies or cakes.

CAROB DATE ICING

In blender, process:

$\frac{3}{4}$ cup water	$\frac{1}{3}$ cup date pieces
$\frac{1}{4}$ tsp. stevia	$\frac{1}{4}$ cup carob powder

Pour into small saucepan and bring to a boil over medium heat.

Combine:
$\frac{1}{4}$ cup white grape juice concentrate or water
1 Tbsp. cornstarch or clear jel

Stir into boiling carob mixture.
Cook, stirring constantly for 5 minutes.
Spread over cake or cupcakes immediately, while hot.

Cookies
Brownies
and Bars

BANANA BARS

Delicious!

In small bowl, whip until soft peaks form:
2 egg whites

Set aside.

In mixer bowl, beat:

2 egg yolks	1 Tbsp. lemon juice
½ cup olive oil	½ tsp. vanilla
1¼ cups mashed ripe bananas	

Add:

1½ cups whole grain flour	1 tsp. stevia
1 tsp. baking soda	

Mix until just combined.
Fold in egg whites.

Fold In:
½ cup chopped walnuts

Pour into 8 x 12" greased pan.
Bake 350° F. for 50 minutes.

CAROB BROWNIES

Beat:

2 eggs	2 tsp. vanilla
¾ cup apple butter	

Add:

1 cup whole grain flour	1 tsp. stevia
½ cup carob powder	1 tsp. baking powder

Mix until just combined.
Spread in greased 8 x 8" pan.
Bake 350° F. for 35 minutes.
Cool and cut into bars.

BROWNIES

In mixer bowl, beat:

1 cup olive oil
4 eggs
1/4 cup apple juice or water

1 cup apple sauce
2 tsp. vanilla

Add:

2 cups whole grain flour
1/2 cup oat bran
1 cup carob powder
1 tsp. baking powder

1 tsp. baking soda
1 tsp. stevia
1 cup chopped nuts

Tip:
Whole grain foods make you feel satisfied quicker with fewer calories.

Combine until just mixed.
Spread on greased jelly roll pan.
Bake 350° F. for 25 minutes.
Cut into bars.

Optional:

When cool, spread Carob Peanut Butter Frosting (page 132) over top.
Cut into bars.

PEANUT BUTTER CAROB CHIP BARS

In mixer bowl, beat:

1 egg
1/4 cup olive oil

3/4 cup unsweetened peanut butter
1 tsp. vanilla

Add:

2 cups whole grain flour
2 tsp. baking powder
1 tsp. stevia

1/2 tsp. salt
1 cup apple juice or water

Mix until just combined.

Fold in:

3/4 cup carob chips

Spread in greased 8 x 12" pan.
Bake 350° F. for 40 minutes.

CHERRY SQUARES

Use Cherry Filling or any canned fruit pie filling.

CHERRY FILLING

In saucepan, bring to a boil:
2 cups sour cherries with juice

Dissolve:
2 Tbsp. cornstarch or clear jel in:
$^1/_2$ cup white grape juice concentrate or water

Stir into cherries. Continue stirring until thickened.

Remove from heat and stir in:
$^1/_2$ tsp. cinnamon

Set aside.

Beat until light and fluffy:
4 eggs

Add:
$^1/_2$ cup apple sauce
$^1/_2$ cup olive oil
1 Tbsp. lemon juice
2 cups whole grain flour
$^1/_2$ tsp. baking powder
1 tsp. stevia

Beat until just combined.
Pour batter onto greased jelly roll pan.
Mark lightly into 12 squares.
Drop 1 rounded Tbsp. of pie filling onto center of each square.
Bake 350° F. for 50 minutes.
Cool. Cut into squares.

CHEWY DATE BARS

Beat:

2 eggs
1 cup apple sauce

2 tsp. vanilla

Add:

2 cups whole grain flour
2 cups rolled oats
2 tsp. baking powder
1 tsp. allspice

1 tsp. nutmeg
1 tsp. cinnamon
1/2 tsp. salt
2 2/3 cups chopped dates

Mix until just combined.
Spread on greased jelly roll pan.
Sprinkle 2 cups chopped walnuts over top and
press down lightly into dough.
Bake 325° F. for 25 minutes.
Cool and cut into bars.

DATE BARS

In blender, process:

2 eggs
2 cups dates

1 cup olive oil
2 tsp. vanilla

Pour into mixer bowl.

Add:

2 cups rolled oats
1 1/4 cups whole grain flour
1 cup oat bran
2 tsp. grated orange peel
2 tsp. baking powder

1 tsp. allspice
1 tsp. nutmeg
1 tsp. cinnamon
1/2 tsp. salt
1 1/3 cups apple juice

Mix until just combined.

Fold in:

1 1/2 cups chopped walnuts

Spread in greased jelly roll pan.
Bake 325° F. for 25 minutes.
Cool. Cut into bars.

FRUIT BARS

Simmer in saucepan for 5 minutes:

1 cup water
1/2 cup chopped dates

1/2 cup raisins
1/2 cup pitted, chopped prunes

Cool.

Beat:

2 eggs
1/4 cup olive oil

1 tsp. vanilla

Add:

1 cup whole grain flour
1 tsp. baking soda
1/2 tsp. stevia
1/2 tsp. cinnamon

1/4 tsp. nutmeg
1/4 tsp. salt
fruit mixture

Mix until just combined.

Fold in:

1/2 cup chopped pecans

Spread in greased 9 x 13" pan.
Bake 350° F. for 25 minutes.
Cool and cut into bars.

ALMOND BARS

In mixer bowl, beat:

1 egg
1/4 cup apple sauce

1/4 cup olive oil
1 tsp. almond flavoring

Add:

2 cups whole grain flour
2 tsp. baking powder

1 1/2 tsp. stevia
1/4 tsp. salt

Mix until just combined.

Fold in:

1/2 cup sliced almonds

Press out thin onto greased jelly roll pan. Bake 325° F. for 25 minutes.
Allow to cool 15 minutes. Cut into bars.

TOFFEE BARS

(Pictured on front cover)

TOPPING

Combine:

1/2 cup walnuts
1/4 cup coconut

1 cup malt sweetened carob chips
1/4 cup olive oil

Set aside.

In blender, process:

1 egg
1/4 cup olive oil

1/2 cup pitted prunes
1 tsp. vanilla

Pour into mixer bowl and add:

2 cups whole grain flour
1 tsp. baking powder
1/2 tsp. salt

1/2 tsp. stevia
1 cup apple juice or water

Mix until just combined.
Pour into greased 8 x 12" pan. Sprinkle topping evenly over cake batter.
Bake 350° F. for 35 minutes. Cut into bars and cool.

PEANUT BUTTER FINGERS

Beat:

2 eggs
2/3 cup unsweetened peanut butter
1/2 cup olive oil

1/2 cup apple sauce
2 tsp. vanilla

Add:

2 cups whole grain flour
2 1/2 tsp. baking soda

1/2 tsp. stevia
1/2 tsp. salt

Beat until just mixed.
Spread on greased jelly roll pan.
Bake 350° F. for 25 minutes.

When cake is almost done baking, melt in heavy sauce pan or double boiler on low heat, stirring constantly:

2 cups malt sweetened carob chips   1 Tbsp. olive oil

Stir in:

2 Tbsp. milk or rice milk

2/3 cup unsweetened peanut butter

Add more milk if too stiff to spread. Spread over bars after removing from oven.
Cut into bars before refrigerating.

BANANA WHOOPIE PIES

In mixer bowl, beat:

2 eggs

2 cups mashed bananas

1 tsp. vanilla

Add:

$3^1/_2$ cups whole grain flour

1 tsp. baking powder

1 tsp. baking soda

$^1/_2$ tsp. cinnamon

$^1/_2$ tsp. cloves

$^1/_4$ tsp. ginger

1 tsp. salt

Mix until just combined. Drop by spoonfuls onto cookie sheet.
(Flatten, or they will rise and make a fat cookie)
Bake 375° F. for 12 minutes.
Ice bottom side of cookie with Carob Date Icing. [page 132 (double recipe)]
Place another cookie on, bottom sides together.   Yields 15 cookies

Tip:
Always remove cookies from cookie sheet immediately after baking.

CAROB MINT FILLED COOKIES

Beat:

1 egg

$^1/_3$ cup olive oil

$^1/_3$ cup apple sauce

1 tsp. vanilla

$^1/_4$ cup water

Add:

$2^2/_3$ cups whole grain flour

$^3/_4$ cup carob powder

1 tsp. baking powder

$^1/_2$ tsp. baking soda

$^1/_2$ tsp. stevia

$^1/_4$ tsp. salt

Mix until just combined.
Roll out on floured surface, $^1/_8$ inch thick.
Cut out with $2^1/_2$ inch cookie cutter. Place on cookie sheet.
Bake 375° F. for 12 minutes.
Cool.

FILLING

Beat until smooth:

8 oz. cream cheese

2 Tbsp. milk or rice milk

$^1/_2$ tsp. peppermint extract

$^1/_2$ tsp. stevia

$^1/_4$ tsp. salt

green food coloring

Spread on half of the cookies. Top with another cookie.

Yields about $1^1/_2$ dozen

ICE CREAM SANDWICHES
Follow Carob Mint Filled Cookies recipe, except roll dough $^1/_{16}$ inch thick. Spread with softened ice cream or Rice Dream Nondairy Dessert in place of cream cheese filling. Freeze.

CAROB CHIP COOKIES

In mixer bowl, beat:
2 eggs
1/2 cup olive oil
1/2 cup apple sauce
1 tsp. vanilla

Add:
2 cups whole grain flour
1 tsp. baking powder
1 tsp. stevia
1/2 tsp. salt

Mix until combined.

Fold in:
1/3 cup carob chips
1/3 cup chopped nuts

Drop by spoonfuls onto cookie sheet. Flatten.
Bake 350° F. for 20 minutes.   Yields 2 dozen

CAROB PEANUT BUTTER COOKIES

In mixing bowl, beat:
3 eggs
1 cup unsweetened peanut butter
1/2 cup olive oil
2 tsp. vanilla

Add:
2 cups whole grain flour
1/2 cup oat bran
1/4 cup carob powder
2 1/2 tsp. baking powder
1 tsp. baking soda
1/4 tsp. salt
1 1/2 tsp. stevia
2/3 cup apple juice or water

Mix.

Fold in:
1/2 cup chopped peanuts

Use a wet spoon to drop dough onto cookie sheet. Flatten.
Bake 375° F. for 12 minutes.   Yields 3 dozen

Spiritual Nugget:
Religion should be our steering wheel, not our spare tire.

CHEWY CAROB OATMEAL COOKIES

In a mixer bowl, beat:

1 egg

1/2 cup apple sauce

1/4 cup olive oil

1 tsp. vanilla

Add:

1 1/2 cups whole grain flour

3 Tbsp. carob powder

1 1/2 tsp. baking powder

1/2 tsp. baking soda

1/2 tsp. cream of tartar

1/2 tsp. cinnamon

1 tsp. stevia

1/2 tsp. salt

Mix until just combined.

Fold in:

1 cup oatmeal

1/2 cup raisins

Drop by spoonfuls onto cookie sheet.
Bake 350° F. for 15 minutes.

Yields 2 dozen

Carob vs. chocolate:
Carob contains only one-hundredth the amount of fat found in chocolate. Carob is rich in calcium.

CAROB DROP COOKIES

In mixer bowl, beat:

1/2 cup olive oil

2 eggs

1/2 cup apple sauce

1 tsp. vanilla

Add:

2 1/4 cups whole grain flour

1/3 cup carob powder

1 1/2 tsp. stevia

3/4 tsp. baking soda

1/2 tsp. salt

2/3 cup apple juice or water

Mix until just combined.
Drop by spoonfuls onto cookie sheet.
Press walnut half into top of cookie. (pictured on page 133)
Bake 375° F. for 12 minutes.

Yields 2 1/2 dozen

COCONUT COOKIES

In mixing bowl, beat:

1/4 cup olive oil   2 tsp. vanilla
1/2 cup apple sauce

Add:

1 3/4 cups whole grain flour   1/2 tsp. stevia
1/2 tsp. baking powder   1 cup unsweetened flaked coconut

On floured surface, roll out 1/4 inch thick.
Cut with a 2 1/2 inch round cookie cutter.
Bake 300° F. for 28 minutes or until edges begin to brown.
Cool.

Melt over low heat, stirring constantly:

1 1/2 cups malt sweetened carob chips
1 Tbsp. olive oil

Drizzle over cooled cookies.
Cool.   Yields 18 cookies

Spiritual Nugget: If God is your co-pilot, trade seats.

CHEWY DATE DROP COOKIES

Delicious!

In blender, process until smooth:

1 egg   1/3 cup olive oil
3 Tbsp. orange juice concentrate   1 1/2 tsp. vanilla
1 cup chopped dates

Pour into mixer bowl.

Add:

1 1/4 cups oat bran   1 1/4 tsp. cinnamon
3/4 cup whole grain flour   1 tsp. cloves
1/2 tsp. baking powder   1/2 tsp. stevia
1/2 tsp. baking soda

Mix until just combined. Drop by spoonfuls onto cookie sheet.
Bake 375° F. for 15 minutes.   Yields 18 cookies

CUT-OUT COOKIES

(Tasty, healthy cut-outs with no butter or lard)

In blender, process:

¹/₄ cup prunes   1 egg

Pour into mixer bowl.

Add:

¹/₂ cup olive oil   1 tsp. cinnamon
2¹/₂ cups whole grain flour   ¹/₂ tsp. ginger
1¹/₂ tsp. baking powder   ¹/₄ tsp. cloves
1 tsp. baking soda   ¹/₄ tsp. salt
1 tsp. stevia

Mix until just combined.

Add:

¹/₄ cup apple juice

On floured surface, roll out to ¹/₄ inch thick.
Dough will crack. Use fingers to press cracks together.
Cut cookies using cookie cutters.
Use spatula to lift cookies to cookie sheet.
Roll out scraps and cut more cookies.
Bake 350° F. for 12 minutes.
Eat as is, or frost with sea foam frosting. (page 132)

Tip:
To keep your
cook book clean:
Slip it into a plastic
bag or cover with
saran before
you begin a
recipe.

NO-BAKE COOKIES

Combine in a small bowl:

2 cups crushed "fruit juice sweetened cornflakes"
¹/₄ cup chopped dates
¹/₄ cup chopped pecans

In a saucepan, combine:

1 cup malt sweetened carob chips
1 Tbsp. olive oil

Stir constantly until just melted.
Remove from heat and stir into cornflakes mixture.
Drop by spoonfuls onto wax paper lined cookie sheets.
Chill until firm.

Yields 2 dozen

SPICY GINGERBREAD COOKIES

In blender, process:

2 eggs

1/4 cup olive oil

2 Tbsp. orange juice concentrate

1/4 cup dried dates

Pour into mixer bowl and add:

2 1/4 cups whole grain flour

3/4 tsp. baking soda

1 Tbsp. cinnamon

2 tsp. ginger

1/2 tsp. cloves

1 tsp. stevia

1/4 tsp. salt

1 tsp. vanilla

1 tsp. maple flavor

> **Cooking from scratch** helps to control fat and sugar content. It also helps to avoid additives.

Beat until just combined.

Roll dough into balls and flatten on cookie sheet.

Bake 375° F. for 12 minutes.   Yields 20 cookies

OUR FAVORITE OATMEAL COOKIES

In a mixer bowl, beat:

1 egg

1/3 cup olive oil

1/2 cup apple sauce

1 tsp. vanilla

Add:

3 cups oatmeal

2/3 cup whole grain flour

1/2 tsp. baking soda

2 tsp. grated orange peel

1 tsp. cinnamon

1/4 tsp. stevia

3/4 cup raisins

Shape dough into balls, flatten, and place on cookie sheet.

Bake 350° F. for 12 - 15 minutes.   Yields 2 dozen

OATMEAL COOKIES

Beat:

¹/₂ cup mashed sweet potatoes   2 Tbsp. olive oil
¹/₂ cup apple sauce   1 tsp. vanilla

Add:

1 cup rolled oats   1 tsp. baking powder
¹/₂ cup oat bran   1 tsp. stevia
1 cup whole grain flour   ¹/₂ tsp. salt
1 tsp. baking soda

Mix until just combined.
Roll dough into balls. Flatten and place on cookie sheet.
Bake 375° F. for 12 minutes.   Yields 18 cookies

PEANUT BUTTER COOKIES

Process in blender until smooth:

¹/₃ cup olive oil   2 Tbsp. water
2 eggs   1 tsp. vanilla
¹/₂ cup prunes

Pour into mixer bowl and add:

1³/₄ cups whole grain flour   ¹/₂ tsp. stevia
1 tsp. baking powder   ¹/₄ tsp. salt
³/₄ tsp. baking soda   ¹/₂ cup unsweetened peanut butter

Mix until just combined. Drop onto cookie sheet.
Flatten cookies, using a fork dipped in water, making criss-cross design.
Bake 350° F. for 15 minutes.   Yields 2 dozen

RAISIN CAROB CHIP COOKIES

In mixer bowl, beat:
1 large egg
1/3 cup olive oil

1/2 tsp. vanilla
3 Tbsp. white grape juice concentrate
                             or water

Add:
1 1/2 cups whole grain flour
3/4 tsp. baking soda

1/2 tsp. stevla
1/4 tsp. salt

Mix until just combined.

Fold in:
1/4 cup carob chips

1/3 cup raisins

Drop by spoonfuls onto cookie sheet.
Bake 350° F. for 12 minutes.

                          Yields 12 cookies

RAISIN OATMEAL COOKIES

Beat:
2 eggs
3/4 cup olive oil

1 tsp. vanilla

Add:
2 cups whole grain flour
1 cup rolled oats
1/2 cup oat bran
1 tsp. baking powder

1/2 tsp. baking soda
2 tsp. cinnamon
1/2 tsp. cloves
1 tsp. stevia

Mix until just combined.

Cookies freeze well.
Bake double batches and freeze part of them for emergencies.

Fold in:
3/4 cup raisins

1/2 cup chopped walnuts

Drop onto cookie sheet.
Bake 350° F. for 15 minutes.

                          Yields 2 dozen

SPICE COOKIES

In mixer bowl, beat:

2 eggs

1 cup apple butter

1 tsp. vanilla

Add:

4$\frac{1}{2}$ cups whole grain flour

1 tsp. baking powder

$\frac{1}{2}$ tsp. baking soda

1$\frac{1}{2}$ tsp. cinnamon

$\frac{1}{2}$ tsp. ginger

$\frac{1}{4}$ tsp. nutmeg

1 tsp. stevia

$\frac{1}{2}$ tsp. salt

$\frac{1}{2}$ cup apple juice or water

Mix until just combined.
Drop onto cookie sheet and flatten.
Bake 350° F. for 12 minutes.   Yields 2$\frac{1}{2}$ dozen

Hint:
Your small or damaged sweet potatoes can be cooked, mashed, and frozen in pint containers for future use.

SWEET POTATO RAISIN COOKIES

Delicious!

Beat:

$\frac{1}{4}$ cup apple sauce

2 eggs

2 cups mashed sweet potatoes

$\frac{1}{4}$ cup water

Add:

2 cups whole grain flour

$\frac{1}{2}$ cup oat bran

1$\frac{1}{2}$ tsp. baking soda

1 tsp. stevia

$\frac{1}{2}$ tsp. cinnamon

$\frac{1}{2}$ tsp. nutmeg

$\frac{1}{2}$ tsp. salt

$\frac{3}{4}$ cup apple juice

1 cup raisins

$\frac{1}{2}$ cup chopped nuts

Mix and drop by spoonfuls onto greased cookie sheet.
Bake 350° F. for 15 minutes.   Yields 3 dozen

THUMBPRINT COOKIES

In blender, process:

1/4 cup dried prunes or dates

1/4 cup apple juice or water

1/4 cup olive oil

2 eggs

1 Tbsp. vanilla

In mixer bowl, combine:

2 1/4 cups whole grain flour

1 tsp. baking powder

1 tsp. baking soda

1 tsp. stevia

1/2 tsp. salt

blender ingredients

Use a wet spoon to shape dough into 1 1/2 inch balls.
Place on cookie sheet.
Dip your thumb into water and make an indentation in the center of each cookie.

LEMON FILLING

Any berry jam can be used in place of lemon filling.

In saucepan, combine:

1/2 cup water

1/4 cup white grape juice concentrate

2 Tbsp. fresh lemon juice

2 1/2 Tbsp. cornstarch

Bring to a boil.

While stirring constantly, add:

1 large egg yolk, beaten

1 tsp. grated lemon peel

pinch salt

Continue stirring until almost boiling.
Remove from heat immediately. Cool.
Spoon 1/2 Tbsp. filling into center of each cookie.
Bake 350° F. for 15 minutes.

Yields 2 dozen

"TOLLHOUSE" COOKIES

Beat:

1/2 cup olive oil

1/2 cup apple sauce

2 eggs

1 tsp. vanilla

Add:

2 cups whole grain flour

1 tsp baking soda

1 tsp. stevia

1 tsp. salt

Mix until just combined.

Fold in:

1 cup carob chips

1/2 cup unsweetened coconut

1/2 cup rolled oats

1/2 cup chopped nuts

Drop by spoonfuls onto cookie sheet. Flatten slightly.
Bake 350° F. for 20 minutes.

Yields 2 dozen

Tip:
Store your spices in alphabetical order to quickly locate the one you are looking for.

ZUCCHINI COOKIES

In mixer bowl, beat:

1 cup apple sauce

1 cup olive oil

3 eggs

2 tsp. vanilla

1 Tbsp. lemon juice

Add:

4 cups whole grain flour

1/2 cup oat bran

2 tsp. baking powder

1 1/2 tsp. stevia

1 tsp. salt

2 cups grated zucchini

1 cup chopped nuts

1/2 cup raisins

Mix until just combined.
Bake 350° F. for 25 minutes.

Yields 3 dozen

Desserts

BAKED APPLES

Cut apples in half. Core and remove stem end, being careful not to remove more apple than necessary from end.
Place apples in baking pan. Fill cavity with orange juice concentrate.
Top with 5 - 6 raisins around edge of cavity.
Bake 375° F. for 45 minutes.

APPLE DATE CRISP

Combine in 9 x 13" baking pan:

8 cups sliced, peeled, sweet apples　　2 cups chopped dates

In a small bowl, combine:

$^1/_2$ cup whole grain flour　　　　$^1/_2$ tsp. stevia
$^1/_3$ cup olive oil　　　　　　　1 cup chopped nuts
1 tsp. cinnamon

Sprinkle over apples.
Bake 375° F. for 40 minutes.　　　　　　Serves 8 - 10

NUTTY BLACKBERRY DESSERT

Process in blender:

4 cups blackberries, raspberries, or blueberries

Bring blackberries to a boil in sauce pan.

Mix together and slowly stir into boiling blackberries:

$^3/_4$ cup water　　　　　　　1$^1/_2$ tsp. stevia
5 Tbsp. cornstarch　　　　　$^1/_2$ tsp. cinnamon

Continue stirring until slightly thickened.
Pour into 8 x 8" baking pan.

TOPPING

Mix together:

1$^1/_2$ cups rice flour　　　　　$^1/_3$ cup olive oil
$^1/_4$ tsp. salt　　　　　　　　$^3/_4$ cup chopped walnuts

Spread over blackberries.

Sprinkle over top:

$^1/_4$ cup chopped walnuts

Bake 350° F. for 35 minutes.
Delicious served with ice cream or Rice Dream Nondairy Dessert.

Serves 6 - 8

PEACH COBBLER

Spread in greased 9 x 13" pan:
8 cups sliced peaches

Sprinkle over peaches:
2 tsp. cinnamon

In mixer bowl, beat:
1/2 cup olive oil   1/2 cup apple sauce
2 eggs

Add:
1 1/2 cups water   1/2 tsp. cream of tartar
1 cup whole grain flour   1 tsp. stevia
4 tsp. baking powder   2 tsp. vanilla

Mix just until combined. Spread evenly over peaches.
Bake 350° F. for 60 minutes.

STRAWBERRY CREAM SQUARES

(Your guests will enjoy this dessert)

Bring to a boil:
1 1/2 cups pineapple juice

Dissolve in 1/2 cup pineapple juice:
2 - 3 oz. boxes sugar free, strawberry jello

Stir dissolved jello into boiling juice.
Remove from heat.

Add:
2 1/2 cups frozen strawberries, sliced in half

Stir until thawed.

Add:
1 1/2 cups drained, crushed pineapple
2 large bananas, diced

Pour half of jello into 8 x 8" pan. Chill until firm.
Leave remaining jello at room temperature.

Tip:
Because of the artificial sweeteners in sugar free jello, we use it only when cooking for guests. For ourselves, we substitute 1 Tbsp. plain gelatin for each 3 oz. box jello.

Spread over chilled jello:
1 cup sour cream or yogurt

Pour remaining jello on top. Chill.

CHERRY DESSERT
CHERRY SAUCE

In saucepan, bring to a boil:

2 cups sour cherries with juice $\frac{1}{4}$ tsp. stevia
1 Tbsp. lemon juice   pinch salt

Dissolve:

3 Tbsp. cornstarch in $1\frac{1}{2}$ cups apple juice

Slowly stir into cherries. Continue cooking and stirring for 2 minutes. Set aside.

BATTER

In mixer bowl, beat:

1 egg   3 Tbsp. olive oil
$1\frac{1}{2}$ tsp. vanilla

Add:

$\frac{2}{3}$ cup whole grain flour $\frac{1}{4}$ tsp. baking soda
$\frac{3}{4}$ cup oat bran $\frac{1}{2}$ tsp. stevia
$\frac{1}{2}$ tsp. finely grated lemon peel $\frac{1}{2}$ cup apple juice
$\frac{1}{4}$ tsp. baking powder

Mix until just combined. Pour cherries into greased $2\frac{1}{2}$ quart casserole. Spoon batter evenly over cherries. Bake 375° F. for 35 minutes.
Allow to cool at room temperature, about 1 hour, for cherries to thicken. Delicious served warm.   Serves 6

FROZEN CRANBERRY BANANA DESSERT

In blender, process until smooth:

2 cups cranberries   3 Tbsp. cornstarch
1 banana $\frac{1}{2}$ cup water
2 Tbsp. white grape juice concentrate   1 tsp. stevia

Pour into sauce pan. Bring to a boil while stirring constantly. Cool.

Add:

1 - 20 oz. can crushed pineapple $\frac{1}{2}$ cup chopped walnuts
2 bananas, sliced

Fold in:

$\frac{1}{2}$ cup egg whites, stiffly beaten

Pour into 8 x 12" pan. Freeze. Allow to soften a little before serving.

RAINBOW JELLO

(Pictured on front cover)

Bring to a boil:

1½ cups pineapple juice ⅛ tsp. salt

Dissolve in ¼ cup white grape juice concentrate:

1 Tbsp. unflavored gelatin

Stir into boiling juice and continue stirring until gelatin dissolves.
Pour half into 8 x 12" pan and refrigerate.
Chill other half until partially thickened, about 1½ hours.
Pour into blender and process on high until fluffy.
Pour over chilled jello.

Repeat from beginning of recipe, three more times, replacing pineapple juice with:

grape juice for second layer
orange juice for third
white grape raspberry juice for fourth.

Note:

Allow juice to cool to room temperature each time before
spooning over previous layer.
Juice can all be thickened and let set at room temperature
until ready for that layer. Chilling may only take 10 - 15 minutes.

Serves 12

Food for
Thought:
Don't fret over
what you'd do with
your time if you could
live life over again –
get busy with
what is left.

RHUBARB DESSERT

In mixer bowl, combine:

1 cup olive oil 1 Tbsp. baking powder
2 cups whole grain flour 1½ cups apple juice or water
1½ tsp. stevia

Pour into greased 9 x 13" pan.

Spread evenly over batter:

3 cups fresh, diced rhubarb

Don't stir.
Sprinkle topping over rhubarb.

TOPPING

Combine in small bowl:

3 Tbsp. olive oil ¼ cup chopped nuts
¾ cup whole grain flour

Bake 350° F. for 55 minutes.

APPLE PIZZA

CRUST

In bowl, combine until crumbly:

4¹/₂ cups whole grain flour
1¹/₂ tsp. salt
1¹/₂ tsp. cinnamon

2 tsp. stevia
³/₄ cup olive oil

Stir in:
³/₄ cup plus 2 Tbsp. water

Divide dough almost in half on floured counter.
Roll out larger half on floured counter. Place in 14" pizza pan.

Sprinkle over crust:
1¹/₂ cups crushed "fruit juice sweetened corn flakes

Arrange in spoke fashion, over entire crust:
¹/₂ inch sweet apple wedges, peeled

Sprinkle cinnamon over apples.
Roll out top crust. Moisten edges of bottom crust.
Cut slits in top crust and fold in quarters. Place on pizza and unfold.
Trim edges. Press edges with fork. Bake 375° F. for 35 - 40 minutes.

CAROB PUDDING

In blender, process:
¹/₄ cup milk or rice milk
2 Tbsp. unflavored gelatin

1 tsp. stevia
¹/₄ tsp. salt

Add:
¹/₂ cup boiling water

Blend for 1 minute or until gelatin is dissolved.

Add and blend until smooth:
¹/₂ cup carob powder
1¹/₄ cups milk or rice milk

2 tsp. vanilla

Pour into mixing bowl and refrigerate until thick.
Scrape pudding away from edge of bowl.

Add:
2 egg whites

Whip on high speed until smooth and fluffy. Pour into serving bowl. Chill.

Serves 4

BREAD PUDDING WITH LEMON SAUCE

In 3 quart casserole, toss together:
6 slices whole grain bread, cubed 1¼ cups raisins

In blender, process:
4 cups milk or rice milk ½ tsp. salt
4 eggs 2 tsp. vanilla
½ tsp. stevia

Pour over bread.
Bake uncovered 350° F. for 1½ hours or until knife inserted in center comes out clean.

LEMON SAUCE

Bring to a boil:
2 cups water 1 tsp. stevia
4 tsp. lemon peel

Dissolve:
5 Tbsp. cornstarch in:
¼ cup white grape juice concentrate
¼ cup lemon juice

Stir into boiling water.
Cook, stirring constantly for 2 minutes.
Serve warm over warm pudding. Serves 8 - 10

Spiritual Nugget: No power can make a man do wrong without his consent.

PINEAPPLE SHERBET

Bring to a boil:
1 cup water

Soak for 5 minutes:
1 cup pineapple juice ¼ tsp. stevia
1 Tbsp. plain gelatin

Stir into boiling water.

Remove from heat and add:
1 cup crushed pineapple 3 mashed, ripe bananas
1 cup milk or rice milk ½ tsp. vanilla

Pour into ice cube trays. Freeze until thick, but not totally frozen.
Drop into blender and process until smooth.
Pour into serving bowl and freeze. Serve partially softened. Serves 6

ICE CREAM DESSERT

Melt in saucepan over medium heat, stirring constantly:

1¼ cups malt sweetened carob chips   ¼ tsp. salt
1 cup milk or rice milk

Remove from heat and set aside to cool.

For crust, combine:

⅓ cup olive oil   ½ cup whole grain flour
1 cup rolled oats

Press into 8 x 8" pan.
Bake 350° F. for 12 minutes. Chill.
Pour carob mixture over chilled crust.
Cover and freeze ½ hour or until firm.

Spread over top:

1 quart ice cream or Rice Dream Non Dairy Dessert, softened.

Sprinkle ½ cup chopped peanuts over top. Freeze.
Remove from freezer and refrigerate 1 hour before serving.

Serves 8

CAROB ICE CREAM TOPPING

Combine in saucepan:

1 cup water   ¼ tsp. stevia
1 cup carob powder

Bring to a boil over medium heat, stirring constantly until smooth.

Add:

2 tsp. vanilla

Drizzle over ice cream or Rice Dream Non Dairy Dessert
and top with chopped nuts.
Store leftover topping in refrigerator.

VARIATION

While still hot, add:

½ cup water   ¼ cup smooth unsweetened
                                              peanut butter

Stir until smooth.
Cool and refrigerate.

PEANUT BUTTER ICE CREAM DESSERT

Delicious!

CRUST

Mix and press into bottom of 8 x 8" square baking pan:

1/3 cup olive oil   1/4 tsp. stevia
1/3 cup oatmeal   1/4 tsp. salt
3/4 cup whole grain flour   1/4 cup chopped peanuts

Bake 350° F. for 15 minutes.
Cool.

Spoon over crust:
2 cups vanilla ice cream or Rice Dream Non Dairy Dessert, softened

Mix:
1 Tbsp. white grape juice concentrate   1/2 cup unsweetened peanut butter

Slowly add, while stirring:
3/4 cup milk or rice milk

Spread half of this over ice cream.
Top with 2 more cups of ice cream, then the rest of the peanut butter mixture.
Sprinkle chopped peanuts over top. Freeze.
Refrigerate 1/2 hour before serving to soften.   Serves 8

STRAWBERRY PINEAPPLE SMOOTHIE

Food for Thought:
If you want a rainbow, you have to have rain.

In blender, combine:
1 cup milk or rice milk
1 cup water
1 cup pineapple juice concentrate
1/2 tsp. vanilla
1/4 tsp. stevia
1 quart whole frozen strawberries

Process until smooth.   Serves 6

BERRY PINEAPPLE SMOOTHIE
Combine in blender:
3 cups frozen raspberries or blackberries
3 frozen bananas
1 cup crushed pineapple, undrained
1 cup orange juice
2 cups milk or rice milk
1/4 tsp. stevia

Process until smooth.   Serves 6 - 8

Tip:
Make your own popsicles
with fruit juice, frozen blender smoothies, shakes, or "Celestial Seasoning" fruit tea. (steeped with stevia leaves)

CITRUS SMOOTHIE
Process in blender until smooth:
3 cups pineapple juice
1 cup orange juice
2 frozen bananas, cut up
2 cups whole frozen strawberries, slightly thawed
1/2 tsp. stevia   Serves 7

PEACH SMOOTHIE
In blender, process until smooth:
1/2 cup milk or rice milk
1 cup orange juice
1 tsp. lemon juice
1 banana
1 quart frozen peaches, slightly thawed
1/2 tsp. vanilla

Pour into glasses to serve.   Serves 6

TROPICAL DRINK
Place in blender:
1 - 12 oz. can frozen orange juice concentrate
2 cups milk or rice milk
1 tsp. lemon juice
1/2 tsp. stevia
2 cups ice cubes

Whiz until ice cubes are finely chopped.   Serves 4

Pies

APPLE PIE

Combine:
4 cups diced, peeled apples
1/2 cup apple juice concentrate
1 tsp. lemon juice
1 Tbsp. whole grain flour
1 tsp. cinnamon
1/2 tsp. nutmeg

Pour into 9" pie shell.
Sprinkle Crumb Topping (page 168) over, or top with another crust.
Bake 400° F. for 40 minutes.

ALMOND PEACH PIE

In kettle, combine:
4 cups fresh peaches
1/4 cup white grape juice concentrate or water
1 tsp. lemon juice
1/8 tsp. almond extract
1/8 tsp. nutmeg
pinch salt
3/4 tsp. stevia

Heat to boiling.

Add:
3 Tbsp. cornstarch dissolved in 1/3 cup cold water

Continue cooking and stirring for 2 minutes.
Pour into pie shell and top with Crumb Topping. (page 168)
Substitute almonds for the nuts.
Bake 350° F. for 25 minutes.

BANANA CREAM PIE

Soften in $\frac{1}{4}$ cup cold water:
1 Tbsp. unflavored gelatin

In blender, process:
1 banana
$\frac{1}{4}$ cup white grape juice concentrate

3 eggs
$2\frac{1}{4}$ cups milk or rice milk

Set aside.

In a saucepan, combine:
$\frac{1}{4}$ cup cornstarch
$\frac{1}{4}$ tsp. stevia

$\frac{1}{4}$ tsp. salt

Over medium heat, stir while pouring in milk and egg mixture.
Continue stirring until hot and bubbly.
Remove from heat. Stir in softened gelatin.

Add:
1 Tbsp. vanilla

Cover tightly and chill.

Add:
3 bananas, sliced

Pile into prebaked 9 inch pie shell.
Sprinkle coconut over top if desired.
Chill.

> **To lift stains from your counter top:** Sprinkle baking soda over stain. Drizzle lemon juice over soda. Let set until stain begins to disappear, about 5 minutes.

BLUE CHERRY PIE

In saucepan, bring to a boil:
1 quart sour cherries

Combine and stir into boiling cherries:
1 cup apple juice
1 tsp. stevia

3 Tbsp. clear jel
pinch salt

Cook and continue stirring for 2 minutes.
Line bottom of unbaked 9" pie shell with fresh blueberries.
Pour cherry filling over.
Bake 350° F. for 35 minutes.
Allow pie to cool before serving. Filling thickens when cold.

CHERRY PIE

Bring to a boil:

1 quart sour cherries, undrained   1 tsp. stevia
³/₄ cup apple juice

Combine and stir in:

¹/₂ cup apple juice   ¹/₄ tsp. almond flavor
6 Tbsp. clear jel   pinch salt
¹/₂ tsp. lemon juice

Bring to a boil and continue stirring for 2 minutes.
Pour into 9 inch unbaked pie shell.
Top with crumb topping. (page 168)
Bake 350° F. for 35 minutes.

LEMON MERINGUE PIE

In saucepan, combine:

1 cup water   ¹/₄ cup fresh lemon juice
¹/₂ cup white grape juice concentrate   6 Tbsp. cornstarch

Bring to a boil.

While stirring constantly, add:

3 egg yolks, beaten   pinch salt
2 tsp. grated lemon rind

Continue stirring until almost boiling.
Remove from heat immediately.
Cool. Pour into cooled Coconut Crust. (page 168)

MERINGUE

Beat until soft peaks form:

3 egg whites   ¹/₄ tsp. cream of tartar
1 Tbsp. white grape juice concentrate   pinch of salt

Pile meringue onto pie filling.
Seal meringue onto edge of crust to prevent shrinking.
Use a spoon to swirl for a pretty design.
Bake 400° F. for 5 minutes or until delicately browned.

Meringue Tip:
Any egg yolk present in the whites will keep the whites from whipping.

PEANUT BUTTER PIE

In mixer bowl, combine:

1 cup unsweetened peanut butter
1/4 cup white grape juice concentrate
1 - 8 oz. package cream cheese, softened

1 tsp. vanilla
1 cup milk or rice milk

Spoon into prebaked pie shell.
Garnish with chopped carob chips. Refrigerate.

FROZEN PUMPKIN PIE

CRUST

In small bowl, combine:

1/2 cup olive oil
1 1/2 cups whole grain flour
1/2 cup rolled oats

1/3 cup chopped peanuts
1/4 tsp. cinnamon
1/4 tsp. nutmeg

Mix together and press into 9" pie pan.
Bake 375° F. for 10 minutes. Chill.

FILLING

Mix together:

1 cup pumpkin
1 tsp. cinnamon
1/2 tsp. nutmeg

1/4 tsp. ginger
1/2 tsp. stevia
1/8 tsp. salt

Add:

1 quart softened vanilla ice cream or "Rice Dream Nondairy Dessert"

Pour into crumb crust. Freeze.

RHUBARB PIE

Beat:

1/4 cup white grape juice concentrate or water   2 eggs

Add:

2 1/2 Tbsp. whole grain flour   2 cups diced rhubarb
1 tsp. stevia

Mix and pour into:

unbaked 8" pie shell

Sprinkle Pie Topping (page 168) over pie.
Bake 350° F. for 50 minutes.

FRESH STRAWBERRY PIE

In saucepan, combine:
1 cup water
$^1/_2$ cup white grape juice concentrate or water
4 Tbsp. cornstarch
2 tsp. unsweetened strawberry or plain gelatin
$^1/_2$ tsp. stevia

Cook over medium heat 5 - 7 minutes, stirring constantly.
Remove from heat. Set aside to cool.

Chop and stir into filling:
6 cups fresh strawberries (leave pieces of strawberries)

Stir well to combine.
Pile into prebaked 9" pie shell.
Chill at least 4 hours before serving.

Hint:
Frozen fruit is available in either quick frozen or dry pack without sugar. Canned fruit can be purchased in water or fruit juice instead of syrup.

STRAWBERRY PIE

Soak for 5 minutes:
$^1/_4$ cup water
1 Tbsp. unflavored gelatin
$^1/_2$ tsp. stevia
$^1/_4$ tsp. salt

Bring to a boil:
2 Tbsp. white grape juice concentrate
1 cup pureed strawberries

Stir gelatin in, stirring until dissolved.
Chill.

When partially set, add:
2 cups sliced, fresh or frozen strawberries

Turn into 8" prebaked pie shell.
Chill.

Hint:
To quickly chill jello or gelatin, set kettle into ice water in kitchen sink. Stir occasionally.

GRAMMY'S SWEET POTATO PIE

CRUST

In bowl, mix together:

1 cup rice or millet flour
1/2 cup fine, unsweetened coconut
1/2 cup walnuts, finely chopped

1/3 cup olive oil
2 Tbsp. water

Press into 9" pie pan.
Bake 375° F. for 10 - 12 minutes.
Cool.

FILLING

Mix in blender:

2 cups cooked sweet potatoes
2 eggs
1 tsp. vanilla
1/4 cup cornstarch

1 tsp. stevia
pinch salt
1/4 tsp. cinnamon
1 1/2 cups hot milk or rice milk

Pour into sauce pan.
Bring to a boil and cook 2 minutes, stirring constantly.

Add:
1/2 cup fine, unsweetened coconut

When cool, pour into baked pie shell.

Top with:
1/2 cup fine, unsweetened coconut   1/2 cup chopped walnuts

Refrigerate.

Note:
To make rice flour, place two cups brown rice in "dry" pitcher of
Vitamix. Process on high speed until fine.
It can also be done in the blender using only one cup of brown rice.
Process on high speed. Blender flour will be a little coarser.

COCONUT CRUST

Combine in bowl:

1 cup rice flour
1/2 cup fine unsweetened coconut
1/2 cup walnuts, finely chopped

1/3 cup olive oil
2 Tbsp. water

Press into 9" pie pan.
Bake 375° F. for 10 - 12 minutes. Cool.

Note:
To make rice flour, place two cups brown rice in "dry" pitcher of Vitamix. Process on high speed until fine. It can also be done in the blender using only one cup of brown rice. Process on high speed. (Blender flour will be a little coarser.)

PIE CRUST

Combine:

1/3 cup olive oil
2 1/3 cups whole grain flour

1 Tbsp. baking powder
pinch salt

Add:

1/2 cup milk or rice milk

Mix just until dough forms a ball. Don't over-mix.
Divide dough in half. Roll out on lightly floured counter.
Fold in half, then in half again. Place in pie pan.
Unfold and press against bottom and sides of pan.
Trim dough around edge of pan.
For prebaked pie shell, prick and bake 375° F. for 15 minutes.

Yields 2 pie shells or 1 double crust

PIE TOPPING

Combine in bowl:

2/3 cup oat bran or rolled oats
2/3 cup whole grain flour

1/4 tsp. stevia
1/4 cup olive oil

Mix well and sprinkle over fruit pie.
Bake according to pie directions.

Yields topping for 1 pie

CRUMB TOPPING

Combine:

1/3 cup olive oil
1 1/2 cups whole grain flour
pinch salt

1/2 cup chopped nuts
1/2 tsp. stevia

Sprinkle over 2 pies and bake, or half of the topping can be kept in refrigerator for up to 2 weeks.

Yields topping for 2 pies

Miscellaneous
and
Snacks

APRICOT ROLLUPS

Combine in kettle:
1¹/₂ cups dried apricots

Cover with water to 1¹/₂ inches above apricots.
Bring to a boil. Simmer covered for ¹/₂ hour.
Drain liquid.

Blend until smooth:
apricots
1 drop almond flavor

Cover 2 cookie sheets with foil, shiny side up.
Brush with olive oil.
Spread ¹/₂ of the fruit mixture on each pan into 12 x 8 inch rectangle.
Bake 200° F. for 3 hours or until dry to touch.
Peel foil off.
With pizza cutter or sharp knife, cut into 1 x 8 inch strips and roll up.
Store in tight container at room temperature.   Yields 2 dozen

CHILI CRACKERS

Tip:
Store bought crackers are high in fat and salt, and usually contain saturated and partially hydrogenated fats.

In mixing bowl, combine:

1 cup yellow cornmeal	¹/₂ tsp. chili powder
¹/₂ cup whole grain flour	¹/₈ tsp. cayenne pepper
³/₄ tsp. salt	3 Tbsp. olive oil
¹/₂ tsp. baking soda	

Add:
¹/₂ cup water

Stir with spoon or use hands to mix until smooth.
Roll out thin on greased jelly roll pan.
Sprinkle dough lightly with paprika.
Cut dough into approximately 2 inch squares.
Cut diagonally through the middle of squares, forming triangles.
Prick crackers with fork.
Bake 350° F. for 25 minutes.
Remove from baking sheet with spatula. Cool on wire rack.
Store at room temperature in an airtight container for up to 1 week.

OAT BRAN CRACKERS

Combine, mixing until crumbly:

2 cups whole grain flour
1 cup oat bran
$1/2$ tsp. baking soda

$1/2$ tsp. salt
$1/4$ cup olive oil
2 Tbsp. apple sauce

Add:

$1/3$ cup apple juice

$1/2$ cup water

Mix well. If too dry and crumbly, add approximately 1 tsp. of water.
Roll out thin on greased jelly roll pan.
Cut crackers into rectangles, using a pizza cutter or knife.
Bake 350° F. for 35 minutes.

Note:
Crackers should always be cut before baking to keep them from breaking easily.

PIZZA CRACKERS

Combine:

1 cup whole grain flour
$1/2$ cup oat bran
1 Tbsp. minced onion
$1/2$ tsp. baking soda
$1/2$ tsp. paprika
$1/2$ tsp. basil

$1/4$ tsp. oregano
$1/8$ tsp. thyme, scant
dash garlic powder
$1/4$ tsp. salt
$1/8$ tsp. pepper

Add:

2 Tbsp. olive oil

Mix well.

Add:

$1/2$ cup pizza sauce

Mix. If dough is crumbly, add more pizza sauce, 1 tsp. at a time
until dough sticks together.
Spread out thin in greased jelly roll pan.
Cut into squares.
Bake 350° F. for 30 minutes.
When cooled enough to handle, separate crackers, turn over, and
bake 300° F. for another 30 minutes.

VEGETABLE CRACKERS

Combine and stir until crumbly:

1 cup oat bran
1 1/2 cups whole grain flour
1 Tbsp. minced onion
1/4 tsp. baking soda
1/4 tsp. celery seed

1/4 tsp. chili powder
1/4 tsp. dill
1/2 tsp. salt
1/8 tsp. pepper
1/4 cup olive oil

Add:

1/2 cup sugarfree ketchup

1 Tbsp. water (more, if too dry)

Mix well.
Roll out thin on jelly roll pan.
Cut with pizza cutter or knife.
Bake 375° F. for 25 minutes.
Cool on wire rack.

Carry a snack with you (such as nuts or seeds) when you go away. Eating at regular times helps avoid those weak, bottomed out feelings which exhaust your adrenals.

CAROB COVERED PRETZELS

In heavy kettle or double boiler, over low heat, melt:

1 cup malt sweetened carob chips
1 Tbsp. olive oil

Stir frequently.
Dip spelt pretzels into melted carob, one at a time, or peanuts, a few at a time. Cool on a cookie sheet.

Note:
Be sure to use malt sweetened carob chips.
Unsweetened carob chips don't melt as well.

CRUNCH

In a bowl, combine:

3 sweet apples, chopped
1 stalk celery, diced fine
1/2 cup peanuts
1/2 cup "fruit juice sweetened cornflakes" or whole grain cereal

Add cereal just before eating or it gets soggy.
Spoon into small individual dishes for a tasty snack.

Serves 6

FRUIT TREATS

Place in food processor or blender:
1/2 cup dried apricots
1/2 cup pitted dates
1/4 cup dried prunes

Process until finely chopped.

Combine in a small bowl:
3 Tbsp. frozen orange juice concentrate
2 Tbsp. olive oil
1 tsp. lemon peel
1/2 tsp. cinnamon
1 1/2 cups chopped pecans, walnuts, or slivered almonds

Add fruit and mix well. *(You may need to use your hands)*
Roll into 1 inch balls. Roll balls in coconut.
Chill.

Roasted, salted nuts should be avoided, as they are high in fat and sodium. Use raw nuts or roast raw nuts at 275° F. for 1/2 to 1 hour, turning twice.

PARTY MIX

In small bowl, mix:
1/2 cup olive oil
1 tsp. paprika
1/2 tsp. celery salt
1/4 tsp. onion powder
1/4 tsp. garlic powder, scant

Tip: We use "Arrowhead Mills" Nature O's cheerios; and "VitaSpelt" spelt pretzels, which contain no sweeteners.

In a large bowl, combine:
10 oz. cheerios
8 oz. pretzels
1 lb. roasted peanuts

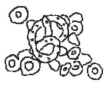

Drizzle oil mixture over.
Toss together.
Spread on baking pan and toast 250° F. for 2 hours, stirring every 20 minutes.

GUACAMOLE

In blender, process until smooth:
1 Tbsp. olive oil
1 cup salsa
1 ripe avocado, peeled (remove seed)
2 cups cooked black beans, drained

Serve with tortilla chips.

TORTILLA DIP

Combine:
1 cup salsa
3/4 cup kidney beans, mashed or blended
1/2 cup sour cream or yogurt, opt.
1/4 tsp. sage
1/4 tsp. basil
salt to taste

Serve warm with tortilla chips.

Popcorn is delicious popped in olive oil.

GOURMET POPCORN

(Pictured on back cover)

Combine in a 3 quart covered bowl:
2 tsp. paprika
1 tsp. chili powder
1 tsp. garlic salt
dash pepper

For less unpopped kernels, store popcorn in the refrigerator.

Add:
8 cups freshly popped popcorn

Cover tightly and shake to evenly coat popcorn.

MUSHROOM CRESCENTS

Allow 8 oz. of cream cheese to soften at room temperature.

DOUGH

In mixing bowl, beat:

1/2 of the cream cheese   1/4 cup olive oil

Add:

2 cups whole grain flour   1/4 cup water
1/8 tsp. salt

Mix until combined. Form into a ball.
Cover and refrigerate until filling is cooled to room temperature.

Meanwhile, in skillet, saute in 2 Tbsp. olive oil until tender:

1 cup finely chopped broccoli   1 Tbsp. finely chopped onion
1/2 cup finely chopped mushrooms

Remove from heat and add:

remaining cream cheese   1/4 tsp. paprika
2 Tbsp. mayonnaise   1/4 tsp. thyme
1/2 tsp. salt   dash pepper

Stir until cream cheese is melted. Cool to room temperature.
Roll out dough on floured surface to 1/8 inch thick.
Cut into 3 inch circles. Place 1 rounded tsp. mix on each circle.
Fold over. Pinch edges to seal.
Brush tops with beaten egg white. Prick tops with fork.
Bake 400° F. for 20 minutes or until browned.
Serve warm.   Yields about 2 dozen

NO-SALT SEASONING

Adding seasoning to food helps you adjust to that bland tasting, low salt or no salt diet.

Combine:

2 tsp. onion powder   1 tsp. thyme
1 tsp. garlic powder   1 tsp. ground mustard
1 tsp. paprika   1/2 tsp. dried parsley

Store in tightly covered container.

For rewards,
don't treat yourself
or your children with
sweets for a job well done.
Find other rewards such
as a "healthy treat" they
seldom receive or doing
something special
together.

TACO SEASONING

In blender, mix:
1/2 cup dried onion flakes
1 Tbsp. dried minced garlic
1 Tbsp. paprika
3 Tbsp. cumin
2 Tbsp. chili powder
1 Tbsp. oregano
1/4 tsp. cayenne pepper
2 Tbsp. cornstarch
1 tsp. salt

Store in tightly sealed container at room temperature.

Tip:
Slice peeled bananas in half lengthwise. Freeze on a cookie sheet. Store in plastic bag after frozen. Enjoy frozen bananas in the summer.

CHEESE (DAIRY FREE)

**Grate over pizza, casseroles,
      or cut cheese sticks for snacks.**

Place in blender and soak 5 minutes:
1 cup boiling water
6 Tbsp. gelatin

Blend just enough to mix.

Add and blend until creamy:
1 cup almonds
1 small garlic clove or 1/8 tsp. garlic powder, optional
1 Tbsp. diced onion
1/2 cup chopped carrot

Add:
1/4 cup nutritional yeast flakes
1 Tbsp. lemon juice concentrate
1/2 tsp. paprika
1 tsp. salt

Blend until smooth, scraping sides.
Pour into greased loaf pan.
Refrigerate.

Note: Extra cheese may be grated and frozen for up to a month.

Nutritional Yeast Flakes
are not the same as baker's yeast.
It gives a cheesy flavor and thickens. Find it in your health food store or food co-op.

Canning
and
Freezing

APPLE BUTTER

Combine:
10 cups thick apple sauce (we prefer Yellow Delicious)
4 cups cider
1 Tbsp cinnamon
$^1/_4$ tsp. cloves
$^1/_4$ tsp. allspice

Bake uncovered in oven at 350° F. for 4 hours or
until desired consistency.
Remove from oven and keep hot on burner.
Lower oven to 200° F. Warm jars and rings in oven.
Cover jar lids with water and bring to a boil.
Pour apple butter into hot jars and seal, one jar at a time.
Turn upside down until cool.

APPLE PIE FILLING

Soak at least 5 minutes:
1$^1/_2$ cups cider   1 cup quick cooking tapioca

Quick Tip:
Apple Crisp
is delicious made
with Apple Pie Filling.
Pour into a pan and top with
Crumb Topping. (page 168)
Bake 350° F. for
40 minutes.

Bring to a boil:
6 cups cider

Add tapioca and continue cooking,
stirring constantly, until thickened and bubbly.
Cook an additional 2 minutes.

Remove from heat and stir in:
1 cup white grape juice concentrate or 1 cup cider and 3 Tbsp. liquid stevia
2 Tbsp. lemon juice
1 Tbsp. cinnamon
$^1/_2$ tsp. nutmeg
1 tsp. salt

Stir this into 35 Yellow Delicious apples, peeled and sliced.
Pack tightly into quart jars, almost to neck.
Cold pack 15 minutes at a rolling boil.   Yields 7 quarts

JAM

**(This jam uses "Pomona's Universal pectin" -
a 100% citrus Pectin. See page 200-201 for suppliers)**

Bring to a boil:
6 cups mashed strawberries, raspberries, or blueberries
1 Tbsp. calcium water (included with pectin)

Meanwhile, mix together:
1 Tbsp. pectin powder
1 tsp. stevia

Add:
$\frac{1}{2}$ cup white grape juice concentrate

Mix well and stir into boiling fruit.
Stir vigorously 1 - 2 minutes to dissolve pectin.
Return to boiling and remove from heat.
Fill freezer containers.
Allow to cool. Freeze.

SYRUP FOR CANNING FRUIT

Combine in pitcher:
8 cups water
$\frac{3}{4}$ cup white grape juice concentrate, opt.
$\frac{1}{2}$ cup stevia syrup

Fill jars with fruit to neck.
Fill jars just to neck with syrup.
Seal and process.

Note:
For canning, use only the green liquid stevia syrup without alcohol, as
fermentation can occur from alcohol or the maltodextrin in the clear stevia.

Tip:
Freeze berries, rhubarb, and zucchini in the amounts you would normally use in a recipe, (such as 2 cups) to eliminate having to measure.

MELON COCKTAIL

Cut into bite size chunks, 1 gallon of each of the following:
watermelon, remove seeds
cantaloupe
honeydew
peaches
2 - 20 oz. cans pineapple tidbits

Gently stir together.
Fill quart jars with fruit. Divide juice from fruit into the jars.
Fill jars just to neck with white grape juice or pineapple juice.
Seal and place in covered canner.
Bring to a rolling boil. Turn burner off.
Remove jars when cool.   Yields approximately 14 quarts

Freezing mint tea: In the summer, just before flower buds open, cut tea. Wash and allow water to evaporate. Pull leaves off stems. Freeze leaves in plastic bags or containers. Tastes almost like fresh tea!

PEAR SLUSH

In large bowl, combine:
24 cups pears, peeled and sliced
3 lb. red seedless grapes
10 bananas, sliced
1 - 20 oz. can crushed pineapple, optional
1 - 12 oz. can white grape raspberry juice concentrate
3 juice cans water

Fill freezer boxes with fruit, evenly dividing juice.
Freeze.
To serve, allow to thaw partially.   Yields 10 quarts

CANNED BEANS

In each quart jar, place:
1½ cups dry beans   1 tsp. salt, optional

Fill to neck with water. Seal.
Pressure can for 90 minutes at 11 lbs. pressure, or cold pack for 3 hours.

CUCUMBER RELISH

Into large bowl, grind:

12 large cucumbers
2 green bell peppers
2 red bell peppers

4 onions
4 stalks celery

Sprinkle 1/4 cup salt over vegetables.
Cover with water.
Allow to set for 1 hour. Drain.

Bring to a boil in a large kettle:

2 cups white vinegar
1/2 cup white grape juice concentrate
2 tsp. celery seed

1 tsp. turmeric
2 tsp. ground mustard
2 tsp. stevia

Add drained vegetables and bring to a boil again.
Simmer for 10 minutes.
Warm jars in 200° F. oven.
Fill and seal. Turn upside down until cool.   Yields 8 - 10 pints

To cold pack: Place sealed jars in canner. Cover with warm water to neck of jar. Bring to a rolling boil. Begin timing. Reduce heat as needed, but keep boiling. Remove jars as soon as time is up.

SALSA

Combine in large kettle or stock pot:

20 cups peeled, chopped tomatoes
4 onions, chopped
8 hot peppers, chopped
3 bell peppers, chopped

1 carrot, chopped
2 stalks celery, chopped
2 Tbsp. chopped parsley
2 garlic cloves, minced

Bring to a boil.

Combine:

1/4 cup vinegar
4 Tbsp. cornstarch

1 tsp. stevia
1 Tbsp. salt.

Stir into boiling tomatoes.
Cook for 20 minutes, stirring occasionally.
Fill jars and seal.
Cold pack for 25 minutes.

PIZZA SAUCE

Use Roma or paste tomatoes for a thicker sauce.

Bring to a boil:
6 quarts tomato juice

Process in blender:

2 onions	4 tsp. oregano
1 quart tomato juice	2 tsp. basil
2 Tbsp. fresh chopped parsley	1 tsp. stevia
2 tsp. garlic powder	4 Tbsp. salt
2 green bell peppers	2 tsp. black pepper
4 hot peppers	

While processing on medium speed, add:
2 cups clear jel or cornstarch

While stirring constantly, pour blender mixture into boiling juice.
Bring to a boil. Simmer uncovered for 2 minutes or until desired thickness.
It will be thicker after it is cooled.
Pour into jars and seal. Cold pack 30 minutes.   Yields 7 quarts

TOMATO JUICE DELUXE

This V-8 juice is what we use in place of tomato juice for everything.

Vegetable amounts can vary. These are approximate.

15 quarts tomatoes, cooked

In kettle, cook covered for 1 hour or until soft:

a few squeezed tomatoes (for liquid)	2 sweet bell peppers, chopped
3 stalks celery with leaves, chopped	1 hot pepper, chopped, optional
4 carrots, chopped	3 sprigs parsley
2 onions, chopped	4 red beet leaves, chopped,
1 garlic clove, chopped	optional

Put tomatoes and vegetables through strainer. Pour in jars.

Add to each jar:

1/2 tsp. salt, optional	1 Tbsp. lemon juice

Seal and cold pack for 20 minutes.

Quick Tip:
After cutting tomato chunks to cook for juice, etc., go in with both hands and squeeze juice out of tomatoes. Saves lots of cooking time!

CANNED TOMATO CHUNKS

Cut stem ends out of tomatoes.
Scald tomatoes by dipping in boiling water for 1 minute.
Slip skins off. If they don't slip off, leave in for a little longer.
If using large tomatoes, cut into chunks.
Pack into quart jars.

If desired, add:
½ tsp. basil
1 tsp. salt
dash of pepper

Seal and cold pack for 45 minutes.

Tip freezing chicken: Cover chicken with water. Cook covered until tender. Allow to set just until cool enough to handle. Debone and chop chicken. Freeze chicken and broth in separate containers.

CANNED MEAT

Tightly pack raw ground or chunk beef or venison into pint or quart jars. Do not add water. For chicken or turkey, tightly pack pieces into jars and fill almost to neck with water.

Add:
½ - 1 tsp. salt to each jar, if desired.

Seal and process in pressure cooker for 90 minutes at 11 lbs. pressure or cold pack for 3 hours.

Note: We like to cover the chicken or turkey with water in a large stockpot and cook until tender. Allow to cool enough to handle, then debone and chop it. Fill jars half way with chicken and fill to neck of jar with broth. Process same as above.

For sandwiches: Grind canned chunk meat. Mix with mayonnaise and diced celery or chopped canned pickles. It can be frozen up to a month.

WHEN TRAVELING

Freeze as much of the food as possible.
Freeze cookies, bars, cake, bread, fruit, etc.
Also freeze meat for sandwiches.
A packed cooler with frozen food can last up to 3 days or more.
Place a layer of newspaper on top of the food, be sure lid fits tightly and cover the whole cooler with a blanket. Take another cooler for fresh produce and your first meals. Remember to remove food ahead of time to thaw.

~~Notes~~

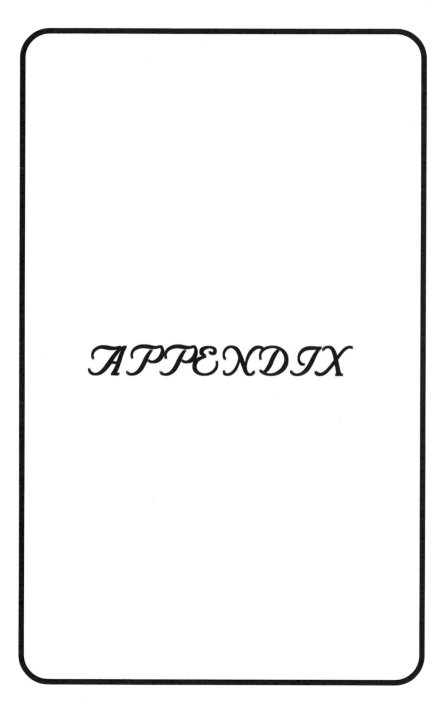

APPENDIX

~~Notes~~

~Low Cholesterol-Low Fat Diet~

We need some fats in our diet, **but** they must be the right kinds of fats. The "bad fats" raise the risk of cancer, whereas the "good fats" help fight cancer.

"BAD FATS"

Saturated fats: Saturated fats include fats from:
> Meats and poultry
> Palm kernel oil
> Fats from dairy products
> Cocoa butter (found in chocolate)

Hydrogenated fats: Hydrogenating turns poly-unsaturated fats into saturated fats by making them more solid. Avoid fats that harden at room temperature.

Hydrogenated fats and partially hydrogenated fats are often found in foods such as:
> Some cereals (check labels)
> Ice cream
> Nondairy creamers
> Salty snacks
> Baked goods
> Some vegetable shortenings

~Low Cholesterol-Low Fat Diet *(Continued)*~

Foods to avoid or use rarely:

Lunch meats	Pork
Fatty cuts of meat	Bacon
Red meat	Sausage
Skin on poultry	Sour cream
Cream	Whipped cream
Butter	Ice cream
Margarine	Cheese
Chocolate	Pastries
Commercial foods	Fried foods
Refined sugar	Refined foods
Fast foods	

Ask your butcher to process your bologna and sausage without adding pork, fat, MSG, or sugar.

Avoid **"Low fat"** - **"Low cholesterol"** foods found in the grocery store. They usually contain **more** sugar (to make them taste better), which contributes to the diabetic epidemic in our country. Don't be tricked into the idea that you can eat more because it is low fat. They are low fat, but high in calories, causing obesity. Many "Low fat - Low Cholesterol" foods contain partially hydrogenated oils.

Avoid fat substitutes such as "Olestra" or "Olean".

Stress can act as a trigger to raise cholesterol.

"GOOD FATS"

<u>Unsaturated fats</u> are good for you! There are two kinds of unsaturated fats:

Mono-unsaturated fats: These fats may help reduce LDL (bad cholesterol) and may raise HDL (good cholesterol) levels. Mono-unsaturated fats include:

Olive oil (very high in mono)   Peanut oil
Almond oil

Poly-unsaturated fats: These fats may help lower total cholesterol levels, but should be used in small amounts. Foods high in poly-unsaturated fats include:

Sunflower oil
Corn oil
Safflower oil
Fatty fish such as tuna, mackerel, and salmon

~Low Cholesterol-Low Fat Diet(Continued)~

The best oil to use is olive oil and should be used as your main oil because it is so high in heart-healthy mono-unsaturated fats.

Foods that help to lower cholesterol:
>Oat bran
>Lentils
>Garlic
>Cod liver oil
>Millet
>Split peas
>Onion
>Fish (mackerel being the highest in
>   Omega-3 fats)
>Beans: pinto, kidney, navy, and black beans

~Egg Free Diet~

Eggs are no longer considered off limits for low cholesterol diets by many physicians. However, they should be used in moderation.

If you have been placed on an egg free diet, here are substitutions you can use.

Flax seed egg substitute:
Grind:
1/4 cup flax seed

Bring to a boil, stirring constantly:
1 1/2 cups water
ground flax seed

Boil for 3 minutes.
Cool and refrigerate in covered container.
2 Tbsp. equals 1 egg.

The following substitutes equal one egg:
1 small to medium <u>banana</u>, mashed
2 Tbsp. <u>thick apple sauce</u>
2 Tbsp. <u>prune butter or prune baby food</u>
1/2 tsp. <u>guar gum</u> + 2 Tbsp. water
1/4 cup <u>tofu</u>
1 Tbsp. <u>arrowroot or cornstarch</u> + 3 Tbsp. water
1 Tbsp. plain <u>gelatin</u> + 2 Tbsp. warm water. Use immediately.

Avoid: Bought baked goods, puddings, cream pies, soft candy, and noodles.

~Adjusting To Less Or No Salt~

       Sodium is one of the nutritional needs of our bodies, but we can get all the sodium we need from our foods as God made them without additional sodium.

       Sodium and table salt are not the same. Table salt is "sodium chloride: and contains 60% or more of chloride. We need to use salt in moderation. Most Americans use far more salt than what is healthy. Diets high in sodium chloride can contribute to kidney, liver, and heart problems including high blood pressure, stroke, and heart disease.

Tips for No Salt Cooking:

- Substitute garlic and onion powder in recipes in place of garlic and onion salt.
- Buy salt free, water-packed tuna, salmon, and mackerel whenever possible.
- Read labels! Watch for salt, sodium, Na, or monosodium glutamate. (MSG)
- Buy frozen vegetables, rather than highly salted canned ones.
- By using waterless cookware and cooking with as little water as possible, more flavor stays in the food.

~Adjusting To Less Or No Salt (Continued)~

- Learn to do your own cooking from "scratch". Many processed foods such as cured meats, canned soups, seasonings, soy sauce, Worcestershire sauce, pickles, condiments, breakfast cereals, salty snacks, and roasted nuts are high in salt.
- Cook food until just tender-crisp. Overcooked, mushy food tastes flat.
- Since commercially canned foods are so high in salt, do your own canning, not using any salt.
- Make your own homemade noodles with out salt.
- Use broth from your home canned or cooked meats to cook pasta, rice, etc.
- Try adding celery, peppers, onion, or garlic to your food. Tomato Juice Deluxe (see recipe page 182) also will make your food tastier.
- When barbecuing, grill your meats plain or brush with salt free butter and/or vinegar.
- Try pineapple juice on chicken; or lemon, orange, or pineapple juice on broiled fish.
- For tastier food try using Mrs. Dash, or hot spices like Cajun.

Check Labels: Some spices and "salt substitutes" have salt or sodium in them.

Some foods with very high salt content: ham, bologna, wieners, sausage, bacon, cheese, and commercially canned soups are just a few.

TIPS FOR LOW SALT COOKING:

- All of the previous "no salt" tips apply to "low salt" cooking too.
- If your canned tuna, salmon, and mackerel have salt added, rinse and drain before using.
- If adding salt to vegetables or potatoes, add it after cooking. The salt is only on the outside surface of the vegetables, requiring less salt, yet giving it a salty taste.
- Do not put the salt shaker on the table.
- Avoid instant hot cereals and most cold cereals.
- Omit or cut in half the amount of salt called for in a recipe.
- Try Bio Salt or Real Salt found in health food stores and food co-ops, or Celtic Salt from The Grain & Salt Society. (see page 203)

~Read Those Labels!~

Make it a habit to always check labels!

Monosodium glutamate (MSG): Eating foods containing MSG may trigger symptoms such as headaches, asthma, or depression. It is added to many packaged and processed foods to enhance their flavor. Many restaurants add MSG to their foods. It may be derived from soy, wheat, or seaweed. <u>MSG is not always listed in the ingredients of foods.</u> "HVP" or "natural flavorings" in foods may contain up to 20% MSG, and not need to be listed. One example is tuna.

Sugar: Watch for: <u>sucrose</u>, <u>glucose</u>, <u>lactose</u>, <u>dextrose</u>, <u>levulose</u>, <u>maltose</u>, <u>karo syrup</u>, <u>corn syrup</u>, <u>corn sweetener</u>, <u>invert sugar</u>, <u>maple sugar</u>, <u>cane sugar</u>, <u>cane syrup</u>, <u>syrup</u>, <u>raw sugar</u>, <u>sorbitol</u>, <u>polysorbate</u>, <u>molasses</u>, <u>honey</u>, and <u>fructose</u>.

BEWARE OF ARTIFICIAL SWEETENERS!
The following is a list of artificial sweeteners to steer clear of as much as possible:

Aspartame (Nutra Sweet) or (Equal) found in beverages, sugar free Jello, and instant pudding.

Acesulfame K found in desserts, candy, chewing gum, beverages, and Sweet One.

Cyclamates

Saccharin found in soft drinks, chewing gum, several table top sweeteners including Sweet'N'Low, Sweet 10, Sugar Twin, and Sweet Mate.

Sucralose found in desserts, beverages, and table top sweeteners.

~Stevia~

Some symptoms of sugar intolerance are: cramps, bloating, canker sores, hyperactive, headaches, dry itchy eyes, depression, low energy, and weak spells.

Stevia is very concentrated, taking only a pinch or a teaspoon in recipes. It is 30 - 300 times sweeter than sugar, depending on the type. It contains no calories and helps balance blood glucose, rather than elevating insulin levels. Stevia is safe for those who have candidiasis as it does not feed yeasts in the intestinal tract. Do some experimenting on your own to obtain the end product you like. Too much may give a sweet off-taste that you don't appreciate.

The FDA has approved stevia as a dietary supplement only. Therefore you will not find the word sweetener on the label. Research shows that it is a very safe substitute for sugar or artificial sweeteners which have side affects and health hazards.

In our recipes, we use <u>green powdered stevia</u> unless the recipe calls for "<u>liquid stevia</u>".

~*Stevia* (Continued)~

It is available in various forms. <u>Dried leaves</u> are excellent for adding to your tea leaves when brewing tea. <u>Green stevia powder</u> is what we use in baking. It is not as sweet as the white stevia. We feel it is the best form for anyone with hypoglycemia or diabetes.

<u>White stevia extract</u> or <u>Stevia Blend</u> is bleached and has other ingredients added. Check the label. It tastes good, but often contains maltodextrin.

<u>Liquid stevia</u> comes in two forms. The green form is closest to nature. The clear form is made from white stevia extract, and as such, often contains maltodextrin.

We use green liquid in syrups for canning because fine green leaves would be noticeable.

Liquid stevia is available without alcohol. If using stevia with alcohol, it is best to add to boiling ingredients to evaporate the alcohol.

For <u>Stevia Conversion Chart</u> see page VIII.

~Whole Grains and Flours~

   Most of these grains can be found at food coops, health food stores, bulk food stores, or check in the "Resources" section for suppliers.

   Whenever possible, buy your grains from a supplier that has a fast turnover and keeps them under refrigeration. Store grains and flour in refrigerator or freezer.
   You might try getting your grains from a local farmer for better prices. If you can get them soon after harvest and store them in a cool place, you will be assured of fresh quality.
   When purchasing baked goods, read labels! "Whole" should be listed in front of the name of the grain. Wheat flour is not whole wheat flour. The dark color may be molasses or artificial coloring.

Barley: a cereal grass, has a bran similar to rice bran. The bran contains all the vitamins, minerals, and oils. Keep refrigerated, as the bran will turn rancid. Pearled barley has part of the bran removed. It is white and almost pure starch. We do not recommend it as most of the nutrition has been removed along with the bran. Barley contains a water soluble fiber, forming bulk which helps to relieve constipation. Barley is low in gluten and will not raise well as a yeast bread. When buying barley, look for hulled barley.

Kamut: an ancient high protein grain - approximately 17% protein, and a relative of durum wheat. It has never been hybridized. Studies have shown that around 70% of people that are sensitive to wheat are able to use kamut. Although it is considered a high gluten flour, it has less gluten than wheat. While that is no problem in most baked goods, yeast breads will have slightly less volume.

~Whole Grains and Flours (Continued)~

Oats: a starchy grain, contains 67.5% carbohydrates and 16.1% protein. It is a good source of vitamin B1, calcium, fiber, and unsaturated fat. When baking, the finished product tends to be a little heavier and wetter. <u>Oat bran is high in fiber.</u> Try using it in baking and cooking. It tends to help stabilize blood sugar imbalances and lowers cholesterol.

Rice: a nutritious grain, contains almost 80% carbohydrates and 8% protein. Use only brown rice. White rice is polished and has the vitamins, minerals, amino acids and fiber removed. Wild rice contains 14% protein and is rich in B vitamins. Rice crops are heavily sprayed. Consider using organic rice, especially if you are sensitive to chemicals. Keep refrigerated.

Rye: a grain high in carbohydrates and contains 5.9% protein. It is often mixed with other grains in bread making.

Spelt: Our preference of whole grain flours is spelt. Spelt is an ancient variety of wheat, but does not cause the problems wheat does. It is easily digested and higher in protein, amino acids, and most minerals than wheat.

Wheat: Modern wheat has been hybridized for higher yield, easier growing and harvesting, and higher gluten content for high-rising fluffy yeast breads. Wheat is considered one of the highest allergy causing foods, possibly due to all the hybridizing. Use whole grain wheat as the bleached refined flours have the bran, germ, and endosperm removed.

~Resources~

AMSTUTZ PANTRY　　　330-857-8159
15893 Baumgartner Rd.
Dalton OH 44618

They ship. Call or write for a price list.

Brown rice, Barley, Dried beans, Lentils

Unsweetened carob chips, Carob powder

Raw nuts and seeds, Unsweetened pure peanut butter

Fruit juice sweetened jam, Sugar free apple butter

Pomona's Universal Pectin, Stevia extract *(white)*

"Real" salt, Whole grain flours, Whole grain pastas

BERRY'S FISH AND HERB FARM　　　937-666-6107
P.O. Box 263
Middleburg, Oh 43336

Stevia extract, Stevia herb, Stevia leaves, Liquid stevia

C. F. SAUER CO.　　　**800-688-5676**
2000 W. Broad Street　　　**804-359-5786**
Richmond VA 23220

Duke's mayonnaise - sugar free; shipped in cases of
4 quarts each.

Call for price quote.

KITCHEN SPECIALTIES AND GRANARY   419-542-6275
09264 Fountain Street Rd.
P.O. Box 100
Mark Center, Ohio 43536

Juicers, Grain mills, Sprouters, Meat grinders, Pasta machines,

Dehydrators, Water distillers; also Beans, Grains, Pasta, Flour, and more.

NATURE'S MARKET   (No mail orders)
4860 E. Main Street, Berlin, Ohio

Rice milk, Soy milk, Malt sweetened carob chips,

Unsweetened carob chips, Carob powder

Sugar free wieners and bologna, Ketchup and Mayonnaise.

Ezekiel bread, Fruit juice sweetened corn flakes, Crispy brown rice

cereal, and many more cereals; Stevia extract, Stevia herb;

Beans, Grains, Nuts, and Seeds in bulk; Sprouting seeds

"Bio" and "Real" salt

POMONA'S UNIVERSAL PECTIN

www.permaculture.net/Pomona/

www.urbanhomemaker.com/items/canning/pomonasuniversalpectin.htm

PURITY FOODS   517-351-9231   FAX: 517-351-9391
2871 W. Jolly Rd.   www. purityfoods.com
Okemos, MI 48864

VitaSpelt Pasta, Grains, Flour, and Pretzels.

Pancake, Muffin, and Bread mixes.

Organically grown beans, Grains, Seeds, Dried fruit, Nuts,
                                                    and more.

SMITH'S BULK FOOD 330-857-1132
5413 S. Mount Eaton Rd.
Dalton, Ohio 44618

They ship. Call or write for price list.

Brown rice, Barley, Dried beans, Lentils

Malt sweetened carob chips, Unsweetened carob chips,
Carob powder

Raw nuts and seeds, Unsweetened pure peanut butter

Fruit juice sweetened jam, Sugar free apple butter

Stevia Extract *(white)*, Stevia Herb *(green)*

Whole grain flours, Whole grain pastas

SMUCKERS

Unsweetened peanut butter, Simply Fruit 100% fruit jam,

R.W. Knudsen pure unsweetened fruit juices.

Available in their retail store at Orrville, Ohio;
in your local grocery; or call 1-800-742-6729 to order.

THE GRAIN AND SALT SOCIETY   1-800-867-7258
273 Fairway Drive   **www.celtic-seasalt.com**
Ashville, NC 28805

Celtic Salt, Grains, Legumes, Pasta, Seasonings, Herbs, Oils,

Butters, Bath and Beauty aids, and more.

VITA-MIX   1-800-848-2649

WAL-MART SUPER CENTER

"Star Kist" Gourmet Choice Tuna

Cold pressed extra virgin olive oil

Juicy Juice Fruit Punch, Rice milk

Unsweetened frozen fruit juice concentrates

Duke's Mayonnaise

~ Making Use of Leftovers ~

Here are some ways to use the more perishable
foods you may have in your refrigerator.

Avocado

Turkey Guacamole Salad 113
Guacamole 174

Bananas, ripe

Apricot Banana Bread 18
Banana Bars 134
Banana Bread 19
Banana Cream Pie 163
Banana Nut Muffins 14
Banana Orange Bread 20
Banana Poppy Seed Dressing 115
Banana Prune Cake 122
Banana Whoopie Pies 140
Citrus Refresher 9
Frozen Cranberry Banana Dessert 154
Peach Smoothie 160
Pineapple Sherbet 157
Strawberry Cream Squares 153

Broccoli

Broccoli Pasta Salad 102
Broccoli Rice Casserole 30
Cream of Broccoli Soup 78
Grilled Veggie Medley 98
Mushroom Crescents 175
Steamed Broccoli 96
Stuffed Baked Potatoes 52
Vegetable Pizza 114

Cauliflower

Cabbage Cauliflower Soup 79
Cream of Cauliflower Soup 79
Creamy Corn Chowder 80
Grilled Veggie Medley 98
Stuffed Baked Potatoes 52
Vegetable Pizza 114

Cream of Mushroom Soup 87

Meat Crust Pie 44
Quick Supper Casserole 52

Eggs, hard cooked

Macaroni Salad 110
Salmon Salad 111
Turkey A La King 64

Fish, cooked

Baked Fish Cakes 71
Fish Pot Pie 50
Garden Salad 108
Stuffed Cabbage Rolls 34
Vegetable Fish Bake 40

Gravy

Pot Pie 51
Use as soup stock in any soup

~ *Making Use of Leftovers* (*continued*) ~

Ground Beef, browned

When browning ground meat, brown as much as will fit in your skillet. Freeze the extra for quick meal preparation.

Chili Mac Casserole 45
Pizza Eggs 6
Pot Pie 51
Spaghetti 57
Spaghetti Squash 59
Taco Pie 63

Lime

Lime & Oil Dressing 117

Mixed Vegetables

You can use bought frozen vegetables, or each time you have leftover vegetables add them to a container stored in your freezer, until you have enough for a recipe.

Royal Dumplings 34
Savory Beef Stew 31
Veggie Rice Casserole 54
Veggie Wild Rice Skillet 59

Mushrooms, fresh

Broccoli Rice Casserole 30
Chicken Spaghetti 57
Cream of Mushroom Soup 87
Fish Pot Pie 50
Mushroom Crescents 175
Oriental Fried Rice 55
Pizza Eggs 6
Pizza Sloppy Joes 90
Rice Stuffed Cornish Hen 35
Spinach Chicken Rollups 70
Stuffed Zucchini 100
Taco Casserole 61
Tuna Tortilla Bake 41
Turkey A La King 64
Vegetable Pizza 114
Yumasetti 65

Oranges

Citrus Marinade 76
Fruit Salads 106,107
Orange Turkey Salad 111

Pineapple, crushed

Berry Pineapple Smoothie 160
Carrot Salad 103
Creamy Pineapple Dressing 116
Pineapple Sherbet 157
Strawberry Cream Squares 153

Potatoes, cooked

Breakfast Pizza 5
Hash browns - browned in olive oil
Pot Pie 51
Potato Salad 112
Quick Supper Casserole 52
Scalloped Potatoes 97
Sour Cream Fish Casserole 47

Potatoes, mashed

Baked Fish Cakes 71
Meat Crust Pie 44
Potato Balls 95
Pumpernickel Bread 25

Sweet Potatoes, cooked

Grammy's Sweet Potato Pie 167
Oatmeal Cookies 146
Sweet Potato Biscuits 12
Sweet Potato Raisin Cookies 148

Pumpkin or Butternut Squash

Frozen Pumpkin Pie 165
Pumpkin Bread 22
Pumpkin Pecan Cake 131

Rice, cooked

Broccoli Rice Casserole 30
Mackerel Pie 72
Stuffed Cabbage Rolls 34
Stuffed Peppers 48
Wild Rice Patties 64

Snow Peas

Carrots & Snow Peas 93
Oriental Fried Rice 55

INDEX

~~Notes~~

BREAKFASTS AND BEVERAGES

BREADS

MAIN DISHES

MEATS

SOUPS AND SANDWICHES

VEGETABLES

SALADS AND SALAD DRESSINGS

CAKES AND CUPCAKES

COOKIES, BROWNIES, AND BARS

DESSERTS

APPLE VIEW PUBLICATIONS
4495 CUTTER ROAD
APPLE CREEK OH 44606

Date:_____

Ship to: Name_____
(Please print)

Street_____

City_____State_____Zip_____

Please send me:

____copies of <u>WOW! Low Cholesterol & Sugar Free Cookbook</u> $ 10.95 each_____

____copies of <u>WOW! This Is Sugar Free Cookbook</u> $ 10.95 each_____
(Making the transition from sugar and refined foods)

____copies of <u>WOW! This Is Allergy Free Cookbook</u> $ 10.95 each_____
(Stevia sweetener & 4-day rotation diet)

Shipping and handling for first book $ 2.50 _____

Shipping for each additional book to same address $ .75 _____

Orders will be shipped parcel post, book rate
(or)   Add extra for UPS $ 1.00 _____

TOTAL _____

Make checks payable to:
APPLE VIEW PUBLICATIONS

Dealers and distributors, write for more information.